"But know this, that in the last days perilous times will come"
                    (2 Timothy 3:1)

This book is dedicated to Lena, my loving wife and best friend.

NO WEAPON

Blood Covenant Protection
In the Last Days

NO WEAPON

*Blood Covenant Protection
In the Last Days*

DR. BRIAN
MILTENBERGER

20 19 18 17   10 9 8 7 6 5 4 3 2 1

No Weapon: Blood Covenant Protection in the Last Days

ISBN-13: 978-1-7325250-0-9

CONTENTS

FOREWORD

⁂

There was a moment in time when everything changed! That was when the first drop of the blood of Jesus touched the mercy seat in heaven. When the perfect blood of the Son of Man touched the perfect altar, a shift took place in the universe. The plan from the foundation of the world was accomplished. The sacrifice was complete, and the way was provided for man to regain his place with his Creator. It was all made possible because of the precious blood of Jesus.

As Jesus took His place as the firstborn among many brethren and as the firstfruits into the kingdom, He also became the Head of a new group called the Church. Jesus was now legally authorized to issue the power of His blood to His body, the Church.

In his new book, No Weapon, Dr. Brian Miltenberger not only explains the power of the blood of Jesus, but how it is to be applied in the life of a believer to bring victory over the attacks of the enemy.

This book is a masterpiece! It is rare to find such deep theological subjects explained in a way that is easy to read and easy to understand. However, Dr. Miltenberger accomplishes the task. As you begin your journey through the pages of this magnificent book, you will be encouraged and strengthened by the truths revealed. When the principles that Dr. Miltenberger reveals are put into practice, you will experience victories and joy in the knowledge that NO WEAPON formed against you will prosper.

This book is a must read and should be in the library of every serious Christian who wants to walk in the freedom and protection of the blood of Jesus.

Dr. Larry Ollison

Author, Pastor, and International Speaker

INTRODUCTION

ભ

I was awakened in the middle of the night by my wife, Lena. The vivid dream she'd experienced several times in the past couple weeks had returned. In the dream, two teenage boys dressed in long black trench coats and carrying assault weapons were chasing students in the school hallway. Lena heard the students screaming frantically as they ran for their lives. Some jumped out of the school's windows to escape. In Lena's dream, the two boys also chased her because they knew she was a Christian.

These disturbing dreams occurred two months before the Columbine massacre on April 20, 1999.

On another occasion, Lena woke me to describe an awful dream she'd just had. She'd dreamed a man was holding a group of people hostage in a room with doors that were chained to prevent escape. The man had two guns, one in each hand, which he used to slay all those in the room. The dream so disturbed Lena, she asked me to stay home with her that day.

Later that afternoon – April 16, 2007 - we heard the tragic news that a gunman had opened fire with two handguns at Virginia Tech University, killing 32 people.

On yet another occasion, I was taking a walk and listening to God's Word on my headphones, when I suddenly felt very disturbed. Just then, I saw hanging from the sky in front of me a huge newspaper. The name of the news organization – *New York Times* – was printed boldly at the top and below were pictures of President George W. Bush and the White House. Suddenly the vision changed to the front page of the *Chicago Tribune*, but the pictures of the President and the White House remained the same. Next came a paper from London, then one from Paris. I knew I was having an open vision of something major about to happen in our nation that would appear on the front page of every newspaper around the world.

This all happened the morning of Tuesday, September 11, 2001, just before the first plane crashed into the Twin Towers.

The LORD knew all along His calling for Lena and me to share what is inside this book – the truth of God's blood covenant of divine protection. What you are about to read can save you, your family, and those close to you. Of course, neither me nor this book will save you, but learning to believe and receive what Jesus has already provided through His blood covenant will ensure that no weapon formed against you will prevail. I pray that the LORD will open the eyes of your heart to receive His blood covenant of divine protection in these perilous times.

CHAPTER 1

❧

UNTOUCHED

Don't you just love reading the Bible? We all love scriptures like, "Blessed are you poor, for yours is the kingdom of God" (Luke 6:20), or "Blessed are you who hunger now, for you shall be filled" (Luke 6:21). But do we also like the scriptures where Jesus tell us, "Blessed are you when men hate you, and when they exclude you, and revile you, and cast out your name as evil, for the Son of Man's sake" (Luke 6:22)? I venture to say that the majority of Christians don't have that verse highlighted in their Bible. Such verses may not be your "favorite" verses, yet they are still vitally important.

> *Love your enemies, do good to those who hate you, bless those who curse you, and pray for those who spitefully use you. To him who strikes you on the one cheek, offer the other also. And from him who takes away your cloak, do not withhold your tunic either. Give to everyone who asks of you. And from him who takes away your goods do not ask them back.*

> Luke 6:27-30

It may seem that Jesus is giving us a commandment that is nearly impossible to fulfill. If someone were to strike you, would you turn the other cheek? Maybe you follow the "Black Eye Rule" - an eye for an eye, a tooth for a tooth, and do whatsoever to them that they havest done unto you. I know our flesh likes that rule a lot better than the Golden Rule! Doing good to those who hate us doesn't sound very appealing. Our flesh has no desire to forgive but craves retaliation. This is why we must renew our minds to the love of God.

Until I really understood the love of God, I did what most people do naturally - whatever feels good, do it and whatever doesn't feel good, don't even bother. So what did Jesus truly teach us? Are we to do good to those who take advantage of us? Are we really expected to forgive those who have insulted or assaulted us? The answer is found in the love of God.

Abiding in the Love of God

In Luke 6, Jesus gives what we call the Sermon on the Mount. In His beatitudes, He taught us how we can overcome persecution by walking in the love of God.

> *Blessed are you when men hate you, and when they exclude you, and revile you, and cast out your name as evil, for the Son of Man's sake. Rejoice in that day and leap for joy! For indeed your reward is great in heaven, for in like manner their fathers did to the prophets.*

Luke 6:22-23

If we truly were commanded to tolerate being violated, then we should employ no form of self-defense. We should use no military force against our enemies. We should do nothing to defend our loved ones against those who would seek to harm them. Can you imagine a battered wife being told, "Honey, I know that he is threatening to knock you upside the head, but remember what

4

Jesus taught us in Luke 6:29. You need to offer up your other cheek." I doubt if she would appreciate your "love lesson."

No loving parent would force their child to put up with being harassed or injured. No caring parent would encourage their precious son or daughter to be battered by a violent stranger for the sake of love. So why would Jesus teach us, "To him who strikes you on the one cheek, offer the other also" (Luke 6:29)? Jesus was teaching His disciples how to overcome hatred with His unconditional love.

During Jesus' earthly ministry, He didn't allow those who hated Him to hurt Him. Not only did He protect Himself from His enemies, He also protected His disciples. The only time Jesus was struck was when He freely offered Himself at the cross. Jesus was beaten and even had His beard plucked out by the Roman soldiers (Isaiah 50:6). But remember, these things happened because He freely gave His life as a ransom for our redemption. Jesus' teaching to "turn the other cheek" was meant to show the Father's unconditional love. No matter how evil your enemies are, you can overcome their hatred by abiding in the Father's love.

> *But I say to you, love your enemies, bless those who curse you, do good to those who hate you, and pray for those who spitefully use you and persecute you.*
>
> Matthew 5:44

When you abide in the love of the Father, it will cause your enemies to be at peace with you: "When a man's ways please the LORD, He makes even his enemies to be at peace with him" (Proverbs 16:7). The love of God dwelling richly in your heart will provide an atmosphere of peace and protection all around you: "You prepare a table before me in the presence of my enemies" (Psalm 23:5). Those who desire to strike or take advantage of you will leave you untouched and unharmed.

Jesus, Son of Man

Jesus lived on this earth just like you and me. He understands what it is like to be human. He was born a human person and not a "super baby." He did not walk on water while growing up. He was not born with super strength and uncanny abilities. He did not operate in His divine powers as the Son of God, but lived as the Son of Man. Had Jesus not been born the Son of Man, the plan of redemption could not have been completed. Yes, He was the Son of God, but He lived on earth as the Son of Man. He emptied Himself of His divine privileges and lived as a human being.

> *Who, being in the form of God, did not consider it robbery to be equal with God, but made Himself of no reputation, taking the form of a bondservant, and coming in the likeness of men. And being found in appearance as a man, He humbled Himself and became obedient to the point of death, even the death of the cross.*

Philippians 2:6-8

Jesus functioned on earth as a human being, just like the rest of us. As a child, He had to have His diapers changed. He had to be nursed. He learned His Hebrew alphabet one letter at a time: *Aleph, Beth, Gimel....* He used natural tools and resources, just like we do. He bathed, urinated, slept, was thirsty, hungry, and got irritated. He knows just how we feel. He knows what it is like to live as a man in a very corrupt and dangerous world. From the moment Jesus was born until He gave His life as a ransom sacrifice, Jesus the Son of Man dwelt safely in the secret place of the Most High. He was surrounded by His enemies, including Satan himself, yet no one could injure Him or take His life. Jesus experienced His Father's divine protection while living in perilous times.

Untouched by Herod the King

I am amazed how many scriptures include promises of divine protection. More than just in Psalm 91, instances of divine protection are found all over the Bible from Genesis to Revelation. In fact, divine protection is even found in the Christmas Story. No, I'm not talking about the story where Rudolph and his friends make it safely to the Island of Misfit Toys. I'm talking about the original Christmas Story, the story of the reason for the season, the birth of our Savior Jesus Christ, the Messiah.

At the time of Jesus' birth, King Herod the Great ruled over Israel. Herod was known to be a very cruel ruler. He was suspicious and fearful and was obsessed with keeping his place of power, regardless of who he had to hurt, torture, or murder to do so. When Herod was in fear of betrayal, he had his own son executed. He had his brother-in-law drowned for treason, then he had his own wife, her mother and her two sons killed.[1] King Herod had the most distinguished residents of Jerusalem slaughtered on the same day of his own death. The strange explanation for his action was that he wanted to make sure the citizens of Jerusalem would be in mourning when he died.[2] King Herod was a real paranoid, psycho, maniac who killed anyone who posed a threat to him – real or perceived.

Herod was very troubled when he heard of the birth of Messiah from the visiting magi (Matthew 2:3). After he learned from the magi the timeframe of the Messiah's birth, he sent them out to find the child, claiming that he, too, wished to go and worship the new Jewish Messiah (Matthew 2:8). The magi found the child and greatly rejoiced, and were about to tell King Herod the location of the child's family. The magi and Jesus' parents had no idea Herod wanted to have the child executed. So how did God protect Jesus and His parents? The magi were divinely warned in a dream that they were not to return to Herod (Matthew 2:12). Not only were the magi warned of Herod's plot, but Jesus' father, Joseph, was also warned. The angel of the Lord appeared to Joseph in a dream instructing him to flee to Egypt: "Arise, take the young Child and His mother, flee to Egypt, and stay there until I bring you word;

for Herod will seek the young Child to destroy Him" (Matthew 2:13). Joseph followed the angel's instructions and the family stayed in Egypt until the death of Herod (Matthew 2:14-15).

When Herod found out that the magi left Israel without notifying him of the child's location, he became infuriated and had all male children executed in Bethlehem and the surrounding areas who were two years old or younger (Matthew 2:16). Jeremiah foretold of the massacre of the young boys of Bethlehem: "A voice was heard in Ramah, lamentation and bitter weeping, Rachel weeping for her children, refusing to be comforted for her children, because they are no more" (Jeremiah 31:15). This is the same prophet Jeremiah who had warned the inhabitants of Jerusalem to repent from their wickedness so they could enjoy God's divine protection. Jeremiah had been imprisoned for prophesying of the coming judgment of God on Jerusalem. He called for the people of Jerusalem to repent and experience divine blessing and safety.

> *In those days and at that time I will cause to grow up to David a Branch of righteousness; He shall execute judgment and righteousness in the earth. In those days Judah will be saved, and Jerusalem will dwell safely. And this is the name by which she will be called: THE LORD OUR RIGHTEOUSNESS.*

> Jeremiah 33:15-16

It was not the will of God for the children of Bethlehem and surrounding areas to be slaughtered by Herod. It was up to the people of Bethlehem to act on their blood covenant right of protection during this time of great persecution. The sovereign will of Father God protected His own Child and He would have responded to anyone else who called on His protection. The people who were in Bethlehem had a blood covenant promise for their entire family to dwell safely from all harm (Jeremiah 33:16).

Just as Father God made sure that Jesus and His parents remained safe underneath the shadow of the Almighty, so also will He keep you and your family safe. So the next time you decorate the Christmas tree and wrap all your gifts, make sure to give thanks to the Father for His divine gift of protection. When you go shopping on Black Friday, you don't have to be afraid of being shot or mugged. You can go to the shopping mall and know that you will remain safe from all danger. The traffic may be heavy and the roads slippery, but you will remain safe under the wings of divine protection. You have nothing to fear, for you are dwelling in the secret place of protection. Declare the promises of divine protection during the holidays rather than singing, "Grandma Got Run Over by a Reindeer." Cover your family with the blood of Jesus while traveling and believe you will make it safely to the other side.

Untouched in His Own Hometown

God's protection continued throughout Jesus' life, including during His earthly ministry as recorded in the four gospels. Did you know that Jesus - kindhearted and tender, unwilling to hurt anybody - had enemies right in His own backyard? If Jesus had enemies, don't be surprised when you have people who despise you. It may be your neighbor, a relative, or even a brother and sister in the Lord.

In Nazareth, the hometown of Jesus, the people of the synagogue were filled with wrath when they heard Jesus preach, and they referred to Him as "Joseph's son" (Luke 4:22). This was not a term of endearment, but an insult. They did not receive Him as a prophet or the Messiah; they rejected Him as a phony. They were outraged at the audacity of Jesus of Nazareth, the son of Joseph.

Jesus responded to the criticism of those in His hometown by saying, "You will surely say this proverb to Me, 'Physician, heal yourself! Whatever we have heard done in Capernaum, do also here in Your country'" (Luke 4:23). Jesus went on to tell them of how God rejected Israel during times of famine and blessed two different Gentiles, Zarephath of Sidon and Naaman the Syrian, because they both believed and received the prophets of the Lord

9

(Luke 4:25-27). The people of Nazareth responded in rage, forcing Jesus out of the city, pushing Him up the hill so they could throw Him over the cliff (Luke 4:28-29). I have had folks get mad at me, but I can't say I made them so mad they wanted to throw me off a cliff! Jesus was treated this way by his own hometown folk; those who knew Him as a good little Jewish boy were now trying to kill Him! That's some serious hometown hatred. But Jesus was kept completely safe as He supernaturally passed through the angry mob untouched and unharmed.

> *Then passing through the midst of them, He went His way.*

> Luke 4:30

Isn't that amazing? Jesus was able to pass through the angry mob like He was invisible. This is an example of what happens when you are in the secret place; you are hidden from the enemy.

Untouched in Jerusalem

This same miracle of divine protection also happened while Jesus was teaching in the temple of Jerusalem. When Jesus proclaimed His divinity to the Jews, "Most assuredly, I say to you, before Abraham was, I AM" (John 8:58), they responded in great wrath by attempting to stone Him to death. Jesus hid Himself from the angry mob and escaped supernaturally.

> *Then they took up stones to throw at Him; but Jesus hid Himself and went out of the temple, going through the midst of them, and so passed by.*

> John 8:59

Notice that Jesus was untouched by the angry crowd. They tried to stone Him, but He was hidden in the secret place of His Father's protection.

Later when Jesus declared, "I and My Father are one" (John 10:30), the Jews were again ready to stone Him. "Therefore they sought again to seize Him, but He escaped out of their hand" (John 10:39). When Jesus once again needed to escape, He was supernaturally shrouded by the angels sent to minister to Him: "These things Jesus spoke, and departed, and was hidden from them" (John 12:36). Isn't our Lord so awesome! Time and again, when the leaders tried to have a "rock concert" to stone Jesus to death, angels hid Him in the secret place. Jesus didn't allow the fiery mob to stone or hurt Him in any way. He trusted in His Father's protection and was untouched.

Untouched by Herod Antipas

Just like King Herod the Great, Herod Antipas also threatened to slay Jesus. The Pharisees warned Jesus to flee from Herod Antipas because he desired to kill Him. Jesus gave Herod a bold message, telling him that he could not kill him because He would give His life as a ransom in Jerusalem.

> *On that very day some Pharisees came, saying to Him, "Get out and depart from here, for Herod wants to kill You." And He said to them, "Go, tell that fox, 'Behold, I cast out demons and perform cures today and tomorrow, and the third day I shall be perfected.' Nevertheless I must journey today, tomorrow, and the day following; for it cannot be that a prophet should perish outside of Jerusalem."*

> Luke 13:31-33

In other words, Jesus was saying, "I cast out demons. I heal the sick. I am in charge. Go tell that fox who thinks he is in charge that he has no power over me."

Jesus was unafraid of Herod Antipas' threats. He stated that no one could take His life, but that He had the power to lay it down and to take it up again as a ransom for sin: "Therefore My Father loves Me, because I lay down My life that I may take it again. No one takes it from Me, but I lay it down of Myself. I have power to lay it down, and I have power to take it again. This command I have received from My Father" (John 10:17-18).

This is where you need to shout, "Hallelujah!" Get a hold of this truth. Jesus has given you the same power so you can declare over your life by faith, "No one can take it from me!" That means no disease can take your life from you. The devil cannot take your life from you. No one and nothing can take your life! You can decree a thing and it shall be established for you (Job 22:28). You can decree, "I shall not die, but live, and declare the works of the LORD" (Psalm 118:17). The religious world will tell you, "Don't say that! You never know what will happen." As a blood covenant believer, you will decree a thing and it shall be established for you according to the Word of God.

Jesus later faced Herod Antipas just before His crucifixion. Herod Antipas had desired to see Jesus for a long time. He hoped that Jesus would do miracles at his command (Luke 23:8). Jesus refused to do any miracles for Herod, nor would He answer any of his many questions (Luke 23:9). Did you know that you don't have to answer to anyone's stupidity? I had someone say to me one time, "If you believe that you can have what you say, then why don't you confess a T-bone steak dinner tonight?" I didn't answer him because Jesus commanded us not to give what is holy to the dogs (Matthew 7:6).

You may have thought that when Jesus taught us to turn the other cheek, He was telling us to do whatever our enemy tells us to do. But Jesus did not teach us to submit to the devil's orders by yielding to our oppressors. He did not call us to be a weak, timid, and passive church. We are called to be mighty warriors, not little church mice. We are never to be intimidated by anyone or anything.

Jesus Was No Wimp

Have you ever gone to church and watched your pastor chase someone out of the building using a bull whip? I'm sure if you did, you would turn around real quickly and find another church! Can you imagine your pastor getting so upset at someone during the church service, that the minister picks up the microphone cord and makes a whip out of it? Did you know Jesus used a whip to drive people out of the temple building? Jesus was no wimp. Jesus cleansed the temple by knocking over the money tables and chasing out all those who were selling merchandise.

> *Now the Passover of the Jews was at hand, and Jesus went up to Jerusalem. And He found in the temple those who sold oxen and sheep and doves, and the money changers doing business. When He had made a whip of cords, He drove them all out of the temple, with the sheep and the oxen, and poured out the changers' money and overturned the tables. And He said to those who sold doves, "Take these things away! Do not make My Father's house a house of merchandise!"*

John 2:13-16

Can you imagine what the headlines would have read in the next day's Jerusalem Post? "Jesus Uses Whip and Overturns Temple Tables!" Jesus did not teach His disciples to be afraid of confrontation. The Bible does not show us a weak and mousy Jesus. The Gospel reveals a warrior Jesus who was not afraid of those who wanted to kill Him.

Jesus exposed Satan's agenda: "The thief does not come except to steal, and to kill, and to destroy" (John 10:10). The Greek word for "destroy" in this verse is *apollumi*, which means "to destroy, to put out of the way entirely, abolish, put an end, to ruin."[4] When Jesus cleansed the temple by overturning the tables of the money changers, the scribes and chief priests wanted to destroy Him: "And the scribes and chief priests heard it and sought how they might destroy (*apollumi*) Him; for they feared Him" (Mark 11:18, insertion mine).

Jesus left the temple and went out of the city of Jerusalem unharmed (Mark 11:19). The enemies of Jesus sought to destroy Him, but He remained safe under His Father's protection.

Untouched by His Enemies

On another occasion, Jesus said to chief priests and leaders, "The stone which the builders rejected has become the chief cornerstone. Whoever falls on that stone will be broken; but on whomever it falls, it will grind him to powder" (Luke 20:17-18). This was not well received by the priests.

Jesus had just told them the story of a man who planted a vineyard. In the story, when the man sent his servant to speak to those who were working the vineyard, the servant was beaten up by the corrupt farmers. When the owner of the vineyard then sent his beloved son to confront the corrupt farmers, they killed him (Luke 20:9-15). Jesus asked the temple leaders a very interesting question, "What will the owner of the vineyard do to them (the corrupt farmers)?" (Luke 20:15, explanation mine). That's a good question isn't it? What do you think will happen to those corrupt farmers who killed the owner's son? Jesus answered His own question, "He will come and destroy those vinedressers and give the vineyard to others" (Luke 20:16).

Knowing that they were the corrupt farmers in Jesus' story, the priests scoffed at Him, "Certainly not" (Luke 20:16). That was when Jesus halted and looked at them with intensity in His eyes: "Jesus didn't back down. 'Why, then, do you think this was written: That stone the masons threw out—It's now the cornerstone!? Anyone falling over that stone will break every bone in his body; if the stone falls on anyone, it will be a total smashup'" (Luke 20:17-18, MSG).

The chief priests and temple leaders were outraged. They had heard enough. They sought to lay hands on Jesus to kill Him but were unable. What stopped them? It was fear. They wanted to kill Jesus, but they were afraid of Him and they feared the people (Luke 20:19).

This wasn't the only time the temple leaders were fuming mad at Jesus. When Jesus healed a man on the Sabbath, they sought to kill Him. However, what really irritated the temple leaders and priests was when Jesus referred to God as His Father. That was the last straw. That made them even more determined that Jesus was a dead man walking.

> *Therefore the Jews sought all the more to kill Him, because He not only broke the Sabbath, but also said that God was His Father, making Himself equal with God.*

> John 5:18

When Jesus went to Judea for the feast, He did it secretly knowing the Jewish leaders desired to kill Him. When some of the residents of Jerusalem saw Him there, they were shocked to see that no one would dare lay hands on Him. Jesus was untouched by His enemies.

> *Now some of them from Jerusalem said, "Is this not He whom they seek to kill? But look! He speaks boldly, and they say nothing to Him. Do the rulers know indeed that this is truly the Christ?"*

> John 7:25-26

> *Therefore they sought to take Him; but no one laid a hand on Him.*

> John 7:30

Jesus preached publicly, unafraid and with boldness, surrounded by those who desired to kill Him: "I know that you are Abraham's descendants, but you seek to kill Me, because My word has no place in you" (John 8:37). Surrounded by those who desired to take His life, Jesus remained untouched by His enemies. He was safe in the secret place of His Father's protection.

This is how you are to live in the midst of your enemies. You have protection in perilous times. There may be someone who has threatened you to instill fear in your heart. When you dwell under the Lord's protection, you'll get the same results Jesus did. No one can touch you. You are untouchable in the secret place. There is nothing to fear when Father God has you covered.

CHAPTER 2

CB

TOUCH NOT MY ANOINTED

In my office, I have an entire collection of Monopoly Collector's Edition games still in their original manufacturer's wrapping. To keep anyone from opening the wrapping, I have a sign posted, "DO NOT TOUCH!" Just in case, I even have the sign posted in Spanish, "No tocar, porfavor." This alerts anyone who may be thinking about opening up my game…don't even think about it! This is vintage stuff!!

Did you know God has a sign over you? It reads, DO NOT TOUCH! You are His valuable, cherished treasure that cost Him His own blood. When you are covered with His blood and dwelling in the secret place, His sign is over you warning the devil, DO NOT TOUCH! The blood covenant assures that the devil cannot touch you.

He remembers His covenant forever, the word which He commanded, for a thousand generations.

Psalm 105:8

He permitted no one to do them wrong; Yes, He rebuked kings for their sakes, saying, "Do not touch My anointed ones, and do My prophets no harm."

Psalm 105:14-15

You may say to yourself, "I'm no prophet! I'm not an anointed one!" You may not be serving in the office of a prophet but if you are born again, you are an anointed one. You have the Anointed One living inside of you.

But you have an anointing from the Holy One, and you know all things.

1 John 2:20

But the anointing which you have received from Him abides in you.

1 John 2:27

The Greek word "Christ" means "Anointed One." If you are a Christian, then you are an anointed one with Christ the Anointed One abiding inside your heart. You are untouchable when it comes to anyone who would try to do you harm.

But he who has been born of God keeps himself, and the wicked one does not touch him.

1 John 5:18

The one who was born of God keeps him safe, and the evil one cannot harm him.

1 John 5:18, NIV

You can point your finger in the devil's face and say, "You can't touch me! I am covered by the blood of Jesus!" The devil can't touch your body, your mind, or your spirit. He can't touch your spouse or your children. He can't touch your health, your wealth, or your stuff. The devil can't touch you, period, because you are covered by the blood of Jesus!

When you are covered by the blood of Jesus, His blood cries out on your behalf, "Do not touch My anointed one!"

Jesus' Disciples Were Untouched

Like Jesus, His disciples were threatened with persecution by those who opposed Jesus' ministry. Yet neither Jesus nor His disciples suffered any harm. Jesus' disciples were untouched by their enemies. They never experienced injury, damage, or loss of life during the three and a half years of Jesus' earthly ministry. Jesus prayed for His Father to protect His disciples from the evil one: "I have given them Your word; and the world has hated them because they are not of the world, just as I am not of the world. I do not pray that You should take them out of the world, but that You should keep them from the evil one" (John 17:14-15). The good news is, Jesus prayed this same prayer for you, too: "I do not pray for these alone, but also for those who will believe in Me through their word" (John 17:20).

"Leave Your Shoes at Home"

Let's put ourselves in the disciples' shoes for just a moment. Let's say that Jesus calls you by name and says, "Follow me." However, this call is predicated on you leaving your shoes at home! I know that when I walk in the mall, I never wear my sandals. I have special shoes I wear that are made for walking. You could say I have the "tender feets." Imagine Jesus requiring you to leave your favorite shoes at home, your Nike, Adidas, or your New Balance! I would be thinking, *Are You kidding me? I just bought a brand new pair of Asics and I have to leave them at home so I can walk barefooted?* What would be the point of that? Yet, this is exactly what Jesus said to His twelve disciples.

When Jesus sent out the twelve, He instructed them to take nothing except their walking stick, shoes and one outfit, "He commanded them to take nothing for the journey except a staff— no bag, no bread, no copper in their money belts— but to wear sandals, and not to put on two tunics" (Mark 6:8-9). Another time, He commanded them to not take any money, no backpacks, no outfits, no walking stick, not even sandals for the journey! "Provide neither gold nor silver nor copper in your money belts, nor bag for your journey, nor two tunics, nor sandals, nor staffs; for a worker is worthy of his food" (Matthew 10:9-10).

Is this radical or what? Why would Jesus tell His followers, "Leave your shoes at home. If you're going to follow Me, you have to be barefooted"? Psalm 91:12 promises that the angels will keep you from injuring your feet: "In their hands they shall bear you up, lest you dash your foot against a stone." Jesus was making the twelve rely on the Father as their only source. Not only did He tell them to leave their sandals but to leave their money, luggage, extra clothes, and walking stick as well. Jesus wanted His disciples to go out and trust in the Father's provision and protection during a time when His ministry was threatened by great persecution.

Commanding Shalom Upon the Home

The Hebrew word for "peace" is *shalom*, which is defined by Strong's Exhaustive Concordance as: "safety, welfare, health, prosperity, peace, rest, all is well, wholeness." The meaning of shalom is also understood to include unharmed and unhurt.[4]

Jesus instructed His disciples that when they entered into a house, to let shalom come upon it.

> *And when you go into a household, greet it. If the household is worthy, let your peace come upon it.*

> Matthew 10:12-13

The shalom of God's peace and protection that rested upon the disciples was released on the households who received their ministry. When they entered into the household, they greeted it with shalom. They were declaring the Lord's peace, safety, protection, wholeness, soundness, and tranquility. When the disciples left the household, the shalom of God's protection remained on the house.

The disciples returned from their ministry journeys safely, reporting to Jesus of all those who were healed and the devils that were cast out (Mark 6:13). Prior to His arrest, Jesus reminded the disciples that when He sent them out, all their needs were met, including their need for protection: "And He said to them, 'When I sent you without money bag, knapsack, and sandals, did you lack anything?' So they said, 'Nothing'" (Luke 22:35).

Every need was met. They didn't lack money without a money bag. They didn't lack clothing without their luggage. And they experienced the same miracle Israel experienced in the wilderness with their feet, "Your garments did not wear out on you, nor did your foot swell these forty years" (Deuteronomy 8:4). When you are dwelling in the secret place, the angels will bear you and your children up so you will not break any bones or injure your feet.

Take Swords with You

Jesus reminded His disciples before His crucifixion that they were under the protection of Father God and did not need earthly weapons. This did not mean, however, that Jesus and His disciples never carried weapons. Jesus later instructed His disciples to be equipped with a money bag, a knapsack, and if any of them was without a sword, to go out and buy one: "Then He said to them, 'But now, he who has a money bag, let him take it, and likewise a knapsack; and he who has no sword, let him sell his garment and buy one'" (Luke 22:36).

Jesus and His disciples were not pacifists. When necessary, they believed in defending themselves, their family, their companions, and their nation with the use of natural weapons. But Jesus wanted His disciples and us to understand that His kingdom is not of this world (John 18:36). Just as Peter and the disciples had to learn to trust in the Lord's protection in the midst of great persecution, so must we.

Beware of Men and Fear Not

Jesus warned His disciples of the great coming persecution from men: "But beware of men, for they will deliver you up to councils and scourge you in their synagogues" (Matthew 10:17). When Jesus told His disciples to beware of men, He was advising them to walk in His wisdom so they could avoid persecution. He was not commanding them to accept persecution, but to avoid it. That's why He said to them, "Beware of men." The disciples were to walk in the wisdom of God, to be wise as serpents among the wolves (Matthew 10:16). They were to follow the voice of wisdom and beware of men who wanted to kill them.

Jesus told the disciples not to fear any man who would threaten them with harm: "Do not fear those who kill the body" (Matthew 10:28). Jesus warned them of upcoming persecution but told them not to fear or worry since the Holy Spirit would give them utterance.

> *You will be brought before governors and kings for My sake, as a testimony to them and to the Gentiles. But when they deliver you up, do not worry about how or what you should speak. For it will be given to you in that hour what you should speak; for it is not you who speak, but the Spirit of your Father who speaks in you.*
>
> Matthew 10:18-20

Was it alright if the disciples worried just a little bit? I mean, it's natural to have some fear when your life is on the line – right? No sir! If you are going to be Jesus' disciple, you cannot tolerate any fear. None. When Jesus tells you to not worry, that means don't worry! Don't fear! That is how you will stay out of the devil's traps - stay out of fear and abide in the hidden place.

Jesus never told the twelve disciples to stay in a city to be killed. Jesus told them to flee to another city when persecuted, "When they persecute you in this city, flee to another" (Matthew 10:23). Sounds like common sense? It's actually the wisdom of God. When Jesus tells you to run, what should you do? RUN!! Don't run in fear. That's only going to signal the devil to chase you. Run in faith, knowing you are safely hidden in the secret place. Jesus assured His disciples that as long as they refused to fear and put their trust in their heavenly Father, they would have all their needs met.

> *Are not two sparrows sold for a copper coin? And not one of them falls to the ground apart from your Father's will. But the very hairs of your head are all numbered. Do not fear therefore; you are of more value than many sparrows.*

> Matthew 10:29-31

You are more valuable to God than any bird, and He takes good care of them. When you know that your Father loves you and will keep you, then fear will not enter your heart.

You are not to fear anything or anyone, no matter how intimidating they may appear. When fear enters your heart, it causes your trust in the Lord's protection to fade away. You start looking to your own strength and abilities as your source of protection. We are not called to be cowardly, but to be courageous and bold as a lion: "But the righteous are bold as a lion" (Proverbs 28:1).

Refuse to Fear

I always enjoy taking walks and relishing the sunny weather of South Florida. One time, I was walking alone downtown listening

23

to God's Word on my headphones. I noticed that in the distance, there was a very tall and muscular man coming toward me. He was shirtless and covered with tattoos. This guy was huge! He looked like the street fighter from Miami known as "Kimbo Slice." I could hear him cursing from far away. He was staring me down with a hard look on his face as he came closer and closer.

Suddenly, he stopped right in front of me. He leaned down and got right in my face just inches away from my nose and shouted, "Hey boy! What're you listen' too?!?" I paused for a moment. In the natural, this man looked like a mountain; but I refused to fear and placed my trust in the Lord. "The fear of man brings a snare, but whoever trusts in the LORD shall be safe" (Proverbs 29:25).

I looked up and shouted back, "I'M LISTENING TO THE WORD OF GOD!!" All of a sudden, the man's countenance changed. It was like he had just got spooked. I don't know what he saw, but he looked above my head and his eyes widened really big, then he turned around and started running the other direction! I just stood there with my mouth open. I thought to myself, I wonder if he saw an angel? I turned around to see if anyone was behind me. I didn't see anyone. It may have been that the Lord allowed him to see an angel who may have been standing right behind me the whole time.

So what would you have done in my situation? Would you have relied on your own strength or skill in street fighting? I know I wasn't about to! Always remember that your confidence is to be in the Lord's strength, not in your own.

> *Cursed is the man who trusts in man, and makes flesh his strength, whose heart departs from the LORD."*

Jeremiah 17:5

When you place your trust in your own strength, you are no longer trusting in the Lord's strength. But when you put all your confidence in the Lord's protection, you will be untouched by those who threaten you.

Blessed is the man who trusts in the LORD, and whose hope is the LORD.

Jeremiah 17:7

Faith in the blood of Jesus is our guarantee that we have a blood covenant with God Almighty for divine protection.

CHAPTER 3

∝

THE BLOOD COVENANT

He shall speak peace to the nations; His dominion shall be "from sea to sea, and from the River to the ends of the earth." As for you also, because of the blood of your covenant, I will set your prisoners free from the waterless pit. Return to the stronghold, you prisoners of hope. Even today I declare that I will restore double to you.

Zechariah 9:10-12

In Zechariah 9:10-12, the Lord is speaking peace to the nations. He is declaring His dominion to the uttermost ends of the earth. The blood of His covenant flows like a river, setting the prisoners free. The stronghold of the Lord's fortress is made available. He wants to restore double to you as you receive His blood covenant.

For He made Him who knew no sin to be sin for us, that we might become the righteousness of God in Him.

2 Corinthians 5:21

There is something very powerful about the blood of Jesus and the way it connects us to God and all His promises. The blood of the holy and spotless Lamb has put you in right standing with a holy, holy, holy God. You have received, by faith in His blood, an abundance of grace and the free gift of His righteousness. God now sees you as if you never sinned. He has given you His righteousness so you may reign in life as a king.

> *Much more surely will those who receive [God's] overflowing grace (unmerited favor) and the free gift of righteousness [putting them into right standing with Himself] reign as kings in life through the one Man Jesus Christ (the Messiah, the Anointed One).*

> Romans 5:17, AMPC

You are to reign in life by the words of your mouth. When you decree a thing, it is to be established unto you (Job 22:28). Christ's blood has made you a king and a priest.

> *To Him who loved us and washed us from our sins in His own blood, and has made us kings and priests to His God and Father.*

> Revelation 1:5-6

You have been marked by the blood of Jesus and declared righteous and are to reign in life. You are to walk in the same dominion and protection as Jesus did when He walked the earth.

Marked by the Blood

When Adam and Eve sinned in the garden, they attempted to cover themselves by sewing fig leaves together. But God clothed them with the skins of animals: "For Adam and his wife the LORD God made tunics of skin, and clothed them" (Genesis 3:21).

God's covering of Adam and Eve's nakedness required the shedding of innocent blood. Later when Adam and Eve's son, Cain, brought an offering to the Lord that was given according to his own efforts and not according to the shedding of innocent blood, it was not accepted: "But He did not respect Cain and his offering" (Genesis 4:5). Both Adam and Cain attempted to cover themselves with the fruit of the ground.

Abel, however, brought a blood sacrifice as his offering to the Lord and it was accepted: "Abel also brought of the firstborn of his flock and their fat. And the LORD respected Abel and his offering" (Genesis 4:4). God required the blood sacrifice as an offering. He explained as much to Cain when He said, "If you do well, will you not be accepted" (Genesis 4:7). But rather than receive the instructions from the Lord, Cain murdered his own brother in anger.

The Lord asked Cain, "'Where is Abel your brother?' He said, 'I do not know. Am I my brother's keeper?'" (Genesis 4:9). The word translated "keeper" is the Hebrew word *shamar*, which means "to guard, to protect, to attend, to regard."[5] Did you know that you are your brother's keeper? You are to exercise dominion to keep you and your brothers and sisters safe in the Lord's protection. A husband is to love his wife the same way Christ loves the Church by protecting her: "For no man ever hated his own flesh, but nourishes and carefully protects and cherishes it, as Christ does the church" (Ephesians 5:29, AMPC).

Cain murdered his brother Abel in anger because Abel had been declared righteous by the blood, while Cain had not (1 John 3:12; Matthew 23:35). Once shed, Abel's blood cried out from the ground for justice. Abel's blood had a voice.

> *And He said, "What have you done? The voice of your brother's blood cries out to Me from the ground."*
>
> Genesis 4:10

The punishment for Cain's sin was that he would be a fugitive and a vagabond wandering the earth. Cain cried out for the mercy of God, "And Cain said to the LORD, 'My punishment is greater than I can bear! Surely You have driven me out this day from the face of the ground; I shall be hidden from Your face; I shall be a fugitive and a vagabond on the earth, and it will happen that anyone who finds me will kill me'" (Genesis 4:13-14).

In response to Cain's plea, God displayed His abundant mercy by providing Cain divine protection from judgment. He marked Cain to keep him from being slain: "And the LORD said to him, 'Therefore, whoever kills Cain, vengeance shall be taken on him sevenfold.' And the LORD set a mark on Cain, lest anyone finding him should kill him" (Genesis 4:15).

The specifics of this mark are unclear. The Hebrew preposition translated "on" is often translated as "for." This verse may be better translated as "And the LORD put (or placed) a mark *for* Cain, lest anyone finding him should kill him." Such a translation would indicate that God "marked" something for Cain's protection. God may have created a physical mark of protection that Cain's enemies would recognize or possibly He placed an invisible sign on Cain that both angels and demons would identify.[6] Either way, Cain was marked with divine protection by the Lord. The mark on Cain was a covenant sign of God's protection and mercy given to someone who did not deserve it. None of us deserve the blessings of God. It is by faith in Christ Jesus that we are deemed worthy of His inheritance.

New Creation Identity

When I started preaching, it was in maximum security prisons. It was amazing how God's Word changed the hearts of the inmates. They no longer saw themselves as prisoners behind bars but as "prisoners of hope" (Zechariah 9:11-12). On the authority of God's Word, they identified themselves as new creations. They knew they had been washed blameless by the blood of Jesus and had been justified.

Therefore, if anyone is in Christ, he is a new creation; old things have passed away; behold, all things have become new.

2 Corinthians 5:17

The world may see you through the eyes of your past, but God sees you through His Son Jesus. You are identified with Christ and that means you are declared righteous, blameless, as if you never sinned. Regardless of your past, you have been marked by God in His mercy.

The LORD is gracious and full of compassion, slow to anger and great in mercy. The LORD is good to all; and His tender mercies are over all His works.

Psalm 145:8-9

So what marks us with divine protection? It is our faith in the blood of Jesus that gives us access to His promise of protection. When you are covered by the precious blood of Christ, you are marked by the Lord. You are a new creation without blemish or spot.

Knowing that you were not redeemed with corruptible things, like silver or gold, from your aimless conduct received by tradition from your fathers, but with the precious blood of Christ, as of a lamb without blemish and without spot.

1 Peter 1:18-19

The blood covenant of protection is not based on what you have done, but on what Christ did at the cross. His blood covenant is extended toward you according to His abundant mercy, unconditional love, and unmerited favor. When you cover your family with the blood of Jesus, you are not calling for God's judgment, but for His mercy. When your children go to school, to the mall or start driving a car, cover them with the blood of Jesus, which brings divine protection. The mark of our protection is solely based upon faith in the blood covenant of Jesus and nothing else.

The Ark of Protection

Noah and his family lived in one of the most dangerous times of history, when giants dwelt on the earth (Genesis 6:4). During this era, the earth was filled with evil and menace.

> *The earth was depraved and putrid in God's sight, and the land was filled with violence (desecration, infringement, outrage, assault, and lust for power). And God looked upon the world and saw how degenerate, debased, and vicious it was, for all humanity had corrupted their way upon the earth and lost their true direction.*

> Genesis 6:11-12, AMPC

God warned Noah that He was going to destroy the earth because it was corrupt and filled with violence (Genesis 6:13), so Noah was instructed by God on how to build the ark: "Make yourself an ark of gopherwood; make rooms in the ark, and cover it inside and outside with pitch" (Genesis 6:14). The danger outside could not penetrate Noah's ark covered with pitch.

The Hebrew word for "pitch" is the root word often translated "atonement." In Hebrew, *kahfar* means "to cover over, atone, or to signify as a place of shelter."[7] This word kahfar is at the root of *Yom Kippur*, which means "Day of Atonement." God established His covenant of protection with Noah and his family; as long as they stayed in the ark, no harm would come to them (Genesis 6:18).

The covenant God made with Noah and his family is a picture of the blood covenant of divine protection that would come through the atonement of the cross. Everyone inside the ark covered with pitch (God's atonement or covering) was kept safe. The blood of Jesus applied over you and your family keeps everyone safe inside the shelter of the Most High. Noah was recognized as being righteous before God (Genesis 7:1), yet his entire family benefited from his covenant with God as long as they remained inside the ark of safety.

The Blood of His Cross

The story of Noah illustrates how the blood of Jesus provides protection for everyone who remains inside the "ark" of protection. When your faith is in the blood, the ark of protection can cover both you and the members of your family. Noah was the only one righteous, yet his entire family remained safe inside the ark. Just as Noah and his family remained safe in the ark that was made of wood and covered with pitch, so you and your family are safe in the ark (the cross) covered with Christ's blood.

Before Noah entered the ark, he was instructed to bring two pair of unclean animals, male and female, and seven each of every clean animal and bird (Genesis 7:2-3). These clean animals were to be used as blood sacrifices for burnt offerings. When he came off the ark, Noah built an altar to God and offered a blood sacrifice of every clean animal and every clean bird as a burnt offering (Genesis 8:20). This is how Noah and his family remained safe even after they came out of the ark. They remained covered by the blood covenant. The Lord smelled the aroma of Noah's blood sacrifice and made an oath to never again curse the ground for man's sake (Genesis 8:21).

The Hebrew name Noah means "rest."[8] When Noah's father, Lamech, named his son, he stated, "This one will comfort us concerning our work and the toil of our hands, because of the ground which the LORD has cursed" (Genesis 5:29). What has brought us peace and rest with God? It is faith in Jesus' blood: "Having made peace through the blood of His cross" (Colossians 1:20).

Noah and his family received God's protection before, during and after the flood. For the year they were in the ark, Noah and his family were never attacked by the creatures that were there with them. It took a supernatural act of God for wild animals to live together without attacking man or each other. The lions, tigers, gorillas, and poisonous snakes all lived on the ark without ever attacking each other or Noah and his family. The divine protection of the Lord was over the ark and all who remained inside.

After the flood and after Noah offered God a burnt sacrifice of the clean animals, the Lord pronounced a blessing on Noah and his sons saying, "And the fear of you and the dread of you shall be on every beast of the earth, on every bird of the air, on all that move on the earth, and on all the fish of the sea. They are given into your hand" (Genesis 9:2). From that day on, every beast on the earth was in fear of Noah and his family. The lion, the bear, and the poisonous serpent never attacked Noah and his family after the flood. Regardless of how treacherous the beasts were during this time, Noah and his family remained unharmed for 350 years after the flood (Genesis 9:28). This is a picture of a family who dwelt safely in the secret place.

The Days of Noah

Paul warned the Church that in the last days, there will be perilous times (2 Timothy 3:1). This verse in the Amplified Bible reads, "But understand this, that in the last days dangerous times [of great stress and trouble] will come [difficult days that will be hard to bear]" (2 Timothy 3:1, AMPC). The Greek word translated "perilous" in this verse is *chalepos*, which depicts "harsh, savage, difficult, painful, fierce, grievous, hard to deal with."[9]

Jesus said that the last days would be like the days of Noah: "But as the days of Noah were, so also will the coming of the Son of Man be" (Matthew 24:37). What were the days of Noah like? They are described as times of great wickedness and violence.

> *Then the LORD saw that the wickedness of man was great in*
> *the earth, and that every intent of the thoughts of his heart*
> *was only evil continually. The earth also was corrupt*
> *before God, and the earth was filled with violence.*

> Genesis 6:5, 11

In spite of what is coming, it is vital for you to not be afraid of living in the last days. Your faith will grow stronger when you know your rights and privileges of divine protection. It is the will of the Father that none in your family perish, but that all come to know His promise of protection.

> *The Lord is not slack concerning His promise, as some*
> *count slackness, but is longsuffering toward us, not willing*
> *that any should perish but that all should come to*
> *repentance.*

> 2 Peter 3:9

In the worst of times, you can know that you and your entire family are protected and secure in the "ark" of the cross and are safe from all dangers that are happening in the world.

Abrahamic Blood Covenant

At the age of 75, Abram, following God's command, left his father Terah, who had served false gods. Abram obediently left the land of his father and because of his faith, God establish a new nation through him, ratifying the promise by a blood covenant. God blessed Abram that he might be a blessing.

> *Now the LORD had said to Abram: "Get out of your*
> *country, from your family and from your father's house, to*
> *a land that I will show you. I will make you a great nation;*

I will bless you and make your name great; and you shall be a blessing."

Genesis 12:1-2

The blood covenant God made with Abram is again described in Genesis 15. In this passage, Abram is told that the Lord will be his shield and protection: "After these things the word of the LORD came to Abram in a vision, saying, 'Do not be afraid, Abram. I am your shield, your exceedingly great reward" (Genesis 15:1). The Lord promised Abram that his children would be like the stars of heaven (Genesis 15:5). God then instructed Abram to bring a three-year-old heifer, a three-year-old female goat, a three-year-old ram, a turtledove and a young pigeon for sacrifice. (The specific mention of three-year-old blood sacrifices is not without significance. The earthly ministry of Jesus, the Lamb of God, lasted just over three years.) God himself cut the animals of sacrifice Abram brought in two down the middle. In a vision, Abram saw a smoking oven with a burning torch (symbols of the presence of God) pass between the halves of the blood sacrifice (Genesis 15:17). The presence of God ratified the blood covenant, confirming for Abram that He was a covenant-keeping God.

The Sign of the Blood Covenant

God changed Abram's name to Abraham, which means "father of many nations," and instructed him to circumcise all males in his household. Circumcision was to be the sign of the blood covenant God made with Abraham.

> *No longer shall your name be called Abram, but your name shall be Abraham; for I have made you as father of many nations. And you shall be circumcised in the flesh of your foreskins, and it shall be a sign of the covenant between Me and you.*

Genesis 17:5, 11

Though circumcision is not uncommon, the act of circumcision is in vain if it is not done by faith in the blood covenant of Jesus Christ.

> *And he received the sign of circumcision, a seal of the righteousness of the faith which he had while still uncircumcised, that he might be the father of all those who believe, though they are uncircumcised, that righteousness might be imputed to them also.*

> Romans 4:11

Faith in the blood of Jesus is our guarantee that we have a blood covenant with God Almighty for divine protection: "By so much more Jesus has become a surety (*guarantee*) of a better covenant" (Hebrews 7:22, explanation mine). This is what separates us from all the false religions of the world; our faith is not in anything or anyone else. We dwell in the secret place of the Most High by faith in the blood of Christ alone. By faith in the blood of Christ, we become sons of Abraham and heirs according to the promise.

> *Therefore know that only those who are of faith are sons of Abraham.*

> *Christ has redeemed us from the curse of the law, having become a curse for us (for it is written, "Cursed is everyone who hangs on a tree"), that the blessing of Abraham might come upon the Gentiles in Christ Jesus, that we might receive the promise of the Spirit through faith.*

> *And if you are Christ's, then you are Abraham's seed, and heirs according to the promise.*

> Galatians 3:7, 13-14, 29

Blood Covenant Benefits and Privileges

There are many benefits and privileges provided to us through faith in the blood. I encourage you to take some time to look these up in your Bible, study and meditate on them. Let the Holy Spirit give you fresh insight into the many benefits of the blood covenant.

We have the remission of sins by the blood of Jesus (Matthew 26:28).

We have been forgiven of all sins by the blood of Jesus (Ephesians 1:7).

We have been cleansed of all sins by the blood of Jesus (1 John 1:7).

We are justified and made righteous by the blood of Jesus (Romans 5:9).

We have peace with our heavenly Father by the blood of Jesus (Colossians 1:20).

We are able to enter into the Most Holy Place by the blood of Jesus (Hebrews 10:19).

We are cleansed of an evil conscience by the blood of Jesus (Hebrews 10:22).

We are made blameless by the blood of Jesus (Hebrews 13:12).

We are perfected forever by the blood of Jesus (Hebrews 10:14).

We can come boldly to the throne of grace by the blood of Jesus (Hebrews 4:16).

We can come near a holy, holy, holy God by the blood of Jesus (Ephesians 2:13).

Our conscience is purged from dead works by the blood of Jesus (Hebrews 9:14).

We have an eternal inheritance through the blood of Jesus (Hebrews 9:15).

We have redemption through the blood of Jesus (1 Peter 1:18-19; Hebrews 9:12).

We are healed by the blood of Jesus (Isaiah 53:3-5).

We are protected by the blood of Jesus (Exodus 12:13; 12:21-23; Isaiah 54:10, 17; Revelation 12:10-11).

We overcome Satan by the blood of Jesus (Revelation 12:10-11).

When you honor His blood,
His blood will honor you.

CHAPTER 4

℃3

FAITH IN HIS BLOOD

I have been in the house of God all my life and I don't regret it, not one day. There is no greater place on earth to be than in the house of God. I remember when I was young, we would sing about the blood of Jesus. We would sing songs like "O the Blood of Jesus," "Nothing but the Blood," and my favorite, "There Is Power in the Blood."

I sang about the blood so much, my grandma, who was the lead pianist at church, told a visiting evangelist about me. During the service, he put a chair behind the pulpit and called me up to the platform. I was only five years old and very small so he had to help me onto the chair, but I stood there and led the congregation in singing about the blood. I still love singing about the blood, but it's one thing to sing about it and another to have a revelation understanding of it.

Revelation Understanding of the Blood

The way you have faith on any subject in the Bible is to first hear and understand what the Word of God teaches. In order to believe in divine protection, you must first hear and understand God's Word. "So then faith comes by hearing, and hearing by the word of God" (Romans 10:17).

You may hear something really good behind the pulpit but still lack understanding of the subject. Israel heard God's Word but lacked understanding. Israel did not heed the Gospel because they lacked revelation understanding of what they heard.

> *But I ask, Have they not heard? Indeed they have; [for the Scripture says] Their voice [that of nature bearing God's message] has gone out to all the earth, and their words to the far bounds of the world. Again I ask, Did Israel not understand?*

Romans 10:18-19, AMPC

For you to have faith in the blood covenant of protection, you must have a revelation understanding of the subject. Over the years, Lena and I have developed a lifestyle of faith and have witnessed many notable miracles because of our faith in the Word, the name, and the blood of Jesus.

Hidden in the Ark

Four hundred years after Joseph died, Jacob's descendants had multiplied from 70 persons to outnumbering the people of Egypt (Exodus 1:5-9). The Egyptians were in fear of Israel long before God performed any miraculous acts of judgment. In dread of the increasing numbers of the Israelites, Pharaoh gave a command to cast every male Hebrew child who was born into the river: "This man (Pharaoh) dealt treacherously with our people, and oppressed our forefathers, making them expose their babies, so that they might not live" (Acts 7:19, explanation mine). This was the first recorded persecution of the Jewish people.

But rather than obey Pharaoh's orders, the midwives of Egypt feared God and protected the male children of Israel (Exodus 1:17). When asked the reason they did not obey Pharaoh's orders, the midwives of Egypt answered, "Because the Hebrew women are not like the Egyptian women; for they are lively and give birth before the midwives come to them" (Exodus 1:19). The way the Israelite women gave birth served as a supernatural sign to the midwives of Egypt that God was on their side, protecting the male children of Israel from premature death.

When Moses was born, his mother hid him to protect him from being fed to the crocodiles. Moses' mother put him in an ark covered with pitch and hid him in the river among the reeds (Exodus 2:3). Smearing the ark with pitch waterproofed it. Just like Noah and his family stayed safe inside the ark covered in pitch, baby Moses also remained safe hidden inside the ark covered in pitch.

Remember that the Hebrew word meaning for atonement comes from the root word "kahfar". On the Day of Atonement, the high priest would present the blood sacrifice for the remission of the sins of Israel (Leviticus 16). The kahfar for you and your family is the blood of Jesus. When you cover your car or your home with the blood of Jesus, you are covered, sealed, and protected by faith in the blood - just like Noah and Moses were safe in their arks covered with pitch. You have been purchased by the blood (Ephesians 1:7), you are cleansed by the blood (Hebrews 9:14), and you and your family remain hidden from destruction by the blood of the Lamb.

> *Then I heard a loud voice saying in heaven,*
>
> *"Now salvation, and strength, and the kingdom of our God, and the power of His Christ have come, for the accuser of our brethren, who accused them before our God day and*

night, has been cast down. And they overcame him by the blood of the Lamb and by the word of their testimony."

Revelation 12:10-11

The daughter of Pharaoh found Moses hidden in the ark on the river. She recognized him as a Hebrew child and yet did not cast him into the water as commanded by her father (Exodus 2:6). When Pharaoh's daughter saw baby Moses crying, she had compassion on him. She commanded the mother of Moses to serve as nurse for her son. The nurse was a hired woman who would breastfeed the infant for at least five years and help raise the child (Exodus 2:9). Moses' mother was paid by Pharaoh's daughter to raise Moses in his early childhood years, when she could train him about the God of Abraham, Isaac, and Jacob (Exodus 2:9-10). This was divine favor working together with divine protection!

When he was grown, Moses saw a Hebrew being beaten by an Egyptian. Moses killed the Egyptian. When Pharaoh learned what Moses had done, He sought to kill him (Exodus 2:15). Moses fled for his safety and dwelled with the Midianites, descendants of Abraham's second wife, Keturah (Exodus 2:21). After the king of Egypt died, God heard the cries of Israel and remembered the blood convent He had made with Abraham, Isaac, and Jacob.

> *So God heard their groaning, and God remembered His covenant with Abraham, with Isaac, and with Jacob. And God looked upon the children of Israel, and God acknowledged them.*

Exodus 2:24-25

Israel, My Firstborn Son

God sent Moses to Egypt to deliver Israel out of slavery. He instructed Moses to tell the new Pharaoh to let His son Israel go.

> *Then you shall say to Pharaoh, "Thus says the LORD:*
> *'Israel is My son, My firstborn. So I say to you, let My son*
> *go that he may serve Me. But if you refuse to let him go,*
> *indeed I will kill your son, your firstborn.'"*

Exodus 4:22-23

God sees you as His son. You may have never considered yourself special in the eyes of God, but know that He is your Father and you are His beloved son. God loves you very much.

> *Behold what manner of love the Father has bestowed on*
> *us, that we should be called children of God!*

1 John 3:1

After being enslaved in Egypt for 400 years, Israel cried out for God to deliver them from slavery and to remember the blood covenant He made with Abraham (Exodus 2:24). God heard the cry of Israel and delivered them: "When we cried out to the LORD, He heard our voice and sent the Angel and brought us up out of Egypt" (Numbers 20:16). Does this mean that God forgot His promise and needed to be reminded of it? We know that omniscient God has no loss of memory, but this is how a blood covenant works between two parties. God expects us to remind Him of His covenant of divine protection.

The Land of Goshen

A blood covenant in ancient times was an agreement between two parties where one party is superior to the other. The everlasting pledge or covenant was ratified between the parties by the ceremonial shedding of blood. When God made a covenant with Abraham's descendants, He promised to provide His protection as the superior party.

God told Moses that the Israelites dwelling in the land of Goshen would be protected from the plagues that He was sending upon Egypt.

> *And in that day I will set apart the land of Goshen, in which My people dwell, that no swarms of flies shall be there, in order that you may know that I am the LORD in the midst of the land. I will make a difference between My people and your people.*

> Exodus 8:22-23

Notice a distinction was made between Israel and Egypt. Upon what was the distinction based? The blood covenant God had made with Abraham and his descendants. Israel cried out for God to honor the blood covenant He had made with their father Abraham. They agreed that upon their deliverance, they would make a blood sacrifice to honor God (Exodus 8:25).

During the fifth plague, the Lord sent severe pestilence upon the cattle and animals of the field. However, a distinction was made between the animals of Egypt and the animals of Israel: "And the LORD will make a difference between the livestock of Israel and the livestock of Egypt. So nothing shall die of all that belongs to the children of Israel" (Exodus 9:4). Even the animals of Israel were protected by the blood covenant God made with Abraham.

After the ninth plague that brought darkness over the land, Pharaoh told Moses, "Go, serve the LORD; only let your flocks and your herds be kept back. Let your little ones also go with you" (Exodus 10:24). Pharaoh agreed to let Israel leave with their children, but required that they leave the animals behind. But Moses refused to compromise the blood covenant Israel had made with God.

> *You must also give us sacrifices and burnt offerings that we may sacrifice to the LORD our God. Our livestock also shall go with us; not a hoof shall be left. For we must take some of them to serve the LORD our God.*

Exodus 10:25-26

Moses knew it was impossible for Israel to serve God without sacrifices of blood. This demand of blood sacrifice was ultimately the distinction between Israel and Egypt. The people of Israel had a blood covenant with God; Egypt did not. Until Israel cried out to God based on the blood covenant He made with their father Abraham, they remained in slavery. Once they put a demand on their blood covenant, God sent a deliverer.

The Blood of the Passover Lamb

The last plague – the plague on the firstborn - required Israel to act on their blood covenant. They were told to shed the blood of an unblemished lamb and smear some of the blood on the doorposts of their houses. What protected Israel during this night of death? Was it because they were Hebrew? No. What prevented the destroyer from killing the firstborn was faith in the Passover lamb. Each household of Israel had covered the crossbeam of the entrance of their house with the blood of the Passover lamb.

Seven-Step Instruction

The Lord gave a seven-step instruction for Israel, in order for there to be divine protection on each house.

#1.   A Lamb for Every Man

First, every man had to take for himself a lamb, according to his household (Exodus 12:3). There was no exception for any household of Israel; all had to make a blood sacrifice. Without the shedding of blood, there would be no covering and thus, no protection on that house. Without the shedding of blood, there is no remission of sins (Hebrews 9:22).

#2. The Lamb Must Be Without Blemish

Second, the lamb to be slain must be a male of the first year without blemish (Exodus 12:5). Jesus is the unblemished Lamb of God who gave His blood (1 Peter 1:19).

#3. The Lamb's Blood Must Be Shed

Third, Israel had to keep the unblemished lamb until the fourteenth day of Nissan and then had to shed the animal's blood at twilight (Exodus 12:6). Notice that the animal's blood had to be shed. If Jesus had not shed His blood for us, we would have no divine protection from death and destruction (Hebrews 9:22).

#4. Place the Blood on the Crosspiece

Fourth, they were to put the blood on the crosspiece of their homes. The crosspiece was comprised of the two beams of the doorpost at the entrance of the house (Exodus 12:7). The Israelites were to take hyssop, a shrub-like plant, dip it in the animal's blood, then strike the crosspiece and lintel of the house (Exodus 12:22). The Passover lamb's blood had to be at the foot of the door, on both sides of the door, and at the top of the door. Picture the entire entrance of each Hebrew's house covered by the blood of the Passover lamb.

#5. Roast the Lamb

Fifth, they were to go inside and roast the lamb with unleavened bread and then eat it with bitter herbs (Exodus 12:8). In preparing the meal, they were not to break any bones of the lamb. Anything not eaten was to be consumed in fire, with nothing left over for the next day (Exodus 12:46). The Messiah's bones were protected and He tasted bitter death for our deliverance and protection: "He guards all his bones; not one of them is broken" (Psalm 34:20).

#6.   Stay Inside the House

Sixth, everyone must stay inside the house until morning (Exodus 12:22). Anyone leaving the house before morning would receive the same judgment as Egypt. Just as Noah and his family stayed in the ark covered in pitch, so Israel had to stay in the house sprinkled with the blood sacrifice. The blood covering the entrance of each house was a seal of protection. This shows the importance of staying under the covering of the blood of Jesus. When you no longer put your trust in the blood of Jesus, the promise of divine protection is made void for you and your family.

#7.   Observe Passover Forever

Seventh, the ordinance of Passover was to be observed by Israel forever (Exodus 12:24). Since the time of the Exodus, Israel has continued to observe Passover on the tenth day of Nissan. When you partake of Holy Communion, you are remembering Jesus, the Passover Lamb of God. The Lord's communion should be honored regularly to recognize our total redemption through the cross. The blood of Jesus is to be honored on a daily basis. When you honor the shed blood of Jesus, all the benefits and blessings provided by His work on the cross are realized for you and your family, including divine protection.

The Blood Distinguishes You

Israel was protected from the death angel because they kept the blood covenant instructions given by God and communicated by Moses and Aaron (Exodus 12:28). Had Israel not heeded to the Lord's instructions, there would have been no distinction between Israel's firstborn and Egypt's firstborn. So it is with us as sons of God. If we do not have faith in the blood covenant promise of protection, there is no distinction between the Church and the world. Divine protection is provided to us freely, but we must receive it by faith. Israel did not have to merit God's protection, but they did have to follow His instructions to receive His divine protection.

When you hear a news report that says, "News Bulletin: There is a thunderstorm warning in your area until this evening with severe winds, hail, and tornadoes possible. Take necessary precaution" – how do you respond? If your only reply is, "We better stay indoors where it's safe," then you are no different than anyone else in your neighborhood. But when you respond with faith in the blood, you distinguish yourself from everyone else.

> *"In the name of Jesus, I cover me, my children, our entire family, our church family, our house, and this neighborhood with the blood of Jesus. I say of the Lord that He is our refuge, our fortress, He is our God and in Him we will trust."*

Six Lanes of Rush Hour Traffic

My mother used to drive herself downtown every morning. One morning she was driving toward downtown in the far right lane when suddenly, a car cut her off. The next thing she knew, she was in an ambulance. She asked, "Where am I? How did I end up here?" The emergency personnel informed her of what just happened saying, "You apparently blacked out and were having a seizure when we found you in the ditch."

The police officer present at the scene told my mother, "If someone would have told me what just happened to you, I would have never believed it!"

My mom asked, "Believe what? All I remember is that I was heading north to work in the far right lane when a car suddenly cut me off. The next thing I know, I am riding inside an ambulance. What just happened?"

The police officer told her, "When you were cut off by the other car, you blacked out. I found your car all the way on the other side of the highway in the ditch, heading south! Somehow your car went all the way from the far right lane heading north, crossed over three lanes of traffic, crossed over the median, crossed over three more lanes of traffic heading toward you in the opposite direction, and somehow landed safely in the ditch on the other side of the highway! If I didn't see it for myself, I would have never believed it! I don't know how you could cross over six lanes of morning rush hour traffic without causing a wreck!"

My mother testified it was the Lord's protection. The only explanation she could give was that her angels had moved her car supernaturally. You may ask, "Do angels know how to drive a car?" I'm sure they do, if necessary. If angels can drive chariots of fire, I'm sure they can drive a Chevy!

My mother is a praying woman of God who learned it from her mother. Our family always was covered by the prayers of Grandma. She was a real watchman of the family for many years. I remember Grandma telling me about my great grandpa, Rev. John F. Bryan, and how he would cover his tent, the people, and the "sawdust trail" with the blood of Jesus. He taught Grandma that there was supernatural power in the blood of Jesus when faith was applied.

When I visited Grandma's house, I would see her every night on her knees in the living room praying in the Spirit. I knew she wasn't praying for her own needs but was always in intercession for someone else. Many people would ask her to pray because she was such a watchman. My mother's angels were on alert because someone had been interceding for her.

When you are driving down the highway and cover your car and the road with the blood of Jesus, you are distinguished from all the rest. When your child gets out of your car and walks to the high school after you cover him or her with the blood of Jesus, your child is distinguished from all the rest. When you cover your family with the blood of Jesus as you ride bicycles together, you are distinguished from all the rest. The highway may be filled with cars moving from lane to lane, but your car is guarded and kept safe by the host of heaven. Why? Is it because you are a Christian? Is it because you went to church this past Sunday? No. That is not what distinguishes you. It is because your faith is in the blood of Jesus. When you honor His blood, His blood will honor you.

SCARLET ROPE OF HOPE

Rahab the harlot had faith in the God of Israel. We know that Rahab, a Gentile, had faith in God's protection because she is mentioned in what many call "The Hall of Faith" – Hebrews 11: "By faith the harlot Rahab did not perish with those who did not believe, when she had received the spies with peace" (Hebrews 11:31).

It was not unusual for Rahab to have men coming in and out of her house daily because she was a harlot. When the king of Jericho sent his men to command Rahab to hand over the two Israeli spies, rather than give the spies up, she risked her own life to hide them. She lied to the king's men, telling them the spies had escaped (Joshua 2:3-5). Rahab then told the two spies that all of Jericho was filled with fear of the God of Israel (Joshua 2:9-11) and requested that in exchange for providing them safety, she and her family be spared when Jericho was destroyed. The two spies made an oath that Rahab and her house would not be destroyed, but the oath was contingent on one thing: She must hang a scarlet rope from her window. If she failed to bind the scarlet rope from her window, she and her family would perish.

The Hebrew word translated "line" or "chord" in Joshua 2 is *tiqvah*, which means "to stretch like a rope." It is also the Hebrew

word meaning "to hope, to have expectation."[10]   Rahab was
instructed to tie a scarlet tiqvah (cord or rope of hope) in her
window with the expectation of being rescued from judgment. It
was no coincidence that the cord Rahab was instructed to use was
scarlet. That scarlet rope of hope symbolized the redemptive work
of Christ that provides divine protection.

You and Your Household

Divine protection was available to Rahab and her family
because of her faith in God. The only condition was that everyone
must remain in her house, which had the token of the scarlet cord
hanging from the window.

> *[Divine protection would not be provided] unless, when
> we come into the land, you bind this line of scarlet cord in
> the window through which you let us down, and unless
> you bring your father, your mother, your brothers, and all
> your father's household to your own home. So it shall be
> that whoever goes outside the doors of your house into the
> street, his blood shall be on his own head, and we will be
> guiltless. And whoever is with you in the house, his blood
> shall be on our head if a hand is laid on him.*

> Joshua 2:18-19, explanation mine

Notice that "whoever" was in the house remained safe. Was
their safety based on their own righteousness? Absolutely not!
They all deserved God's judgment for their ungodliness. The only
thing that qualified Rahab and her family for protection was the
scarlet rope hanging out the window. When you place your trust
in the blood of Jesus, it works for both you and your household:
"She fears not the snow for her family, for all her household are
doubly clothed in scarlet" (Proverbs 31:21 AMPC). As long as
Rahab had faith in the God of Israel, she and her entire household
remained safe. Rahab responded to the spies' instructions,
"According to your words, so be it" (Joshua 2:21).

Rahab's house was constructed upon the city wall: "For her house was on the city wall; she dwelt on the wall" (Joshua 2:15). Having a house located on the city wall may seem unusual, but it was customary during this time for a house to be built within the walls of the city. In this case, however, having a house built within the walls of the city meant that when the walls of Jericho fell, Rahab and her family had to remain in a house situated on those falling walls. Rahab and her family had to remain in the house believing God would protect them, regardless of the dreadful sound of enormous walls collapsing all around them. No matter what you hear, see, or feel, remain under the shadow of the Almighty. Don't vacate with fear. Keep your trust in God's blood covenant and dwell safely in the secret place.

You may be shocked that a woman such as Rahab - a harlot or prostitute – would be included in the "Hall of Faith" of Hebrews 11. After she was rescued in the fall of Jericho, do you think Rahab continue in sin? Of course not. Rahab repented when she encountered the grace of God. When you embrace His grace, you will no longer continue in sin.

When Israel marched around the city of Jericho carrying the Ark of the covenant, before anyone shouted, Joshua gave specific instructions: "Only Rahab the harlot shall live, she and all who are with her in the house" (Joshua 6:17). This divine hedge of protection for Rahab and her family would have never existed had she trusted in anything other than the instructions of the spies when they told her to bind the scarlet rope from her window and remain in the house. This illustrates how God's divine protection is accessible to those who have placed their faith in the blood of Jesus, who remain in the secret place. When your faith is in the blood of Jesus, you and your entire family are encircled by the hedge of God's protection.

Rahab and her house not only were saved from the destruction of Jericho, but they dwelt together with Israel: "And Joshua spared Rahab the harlot, her father's household, and all that she had. So she dwells in Israel to this day" (Joshua 6:25). Rahab and her family were no longer identified as enemies of God but were engrafted with the children of Israel. Rahab was even included in the genealogy of the Messiah (Matthew 1:5)! A former prostitute found a place in God's plan of redemption.

No matter how much you have sinned, the blood of Jesus is greater. Nothing can stop the cleansing blood of Jesus when faith is applied. The Lord is good and His mercy is everlasting.

The Blood Cries "Mercy"

After my wife and I got married, we moved into a small one bedroom apartment in a not-so-quiet neighborhood. The neighbor on our left side played loud hip hop music late at night. We often heard someone getting slapped around and thrown against the wall like they were being beat to death. After about a week of this, I decided to go next door to save the lady from her abusive boyfriend. Just before I knocked on the door, the boyfriend came sailing out of the apartment and landed outside on the ground on his backside. His very huge girlfriend had literally thrown him out. I realized then that all of the beating, bouncing, and slamming was the girlfriend slapping around her boyfriend.

Our neighbor on the right side was a lady involved in prostitution. She had two sweet little girls who lived with her at the time. The mother was always at home during the day and had a different man visiting her every couple of hours. Her customers quickly sneaked in her apartment, stayed an hour, and quickly left. Her daughters watched TV in the living room while their mother was locked in her room with man after man.

Lena and I asked the mother if we could take the girls with us to church on Sunday. She happily agreed, but never wanted to go with us, even though we invited her. One Sunday, she let us know she wanted to go with us and her kids to church. When we got to the service, we sat close to the front. When the altar call was given, she literally ran to the altar, fell on her knees and cried out to God. Even though this lady was a sinner, when she cried out to the Lord, He heard her cry and answered with His saving grace. The blood of Jesus washed away every one of her sins in a moment and set her free from all bondage. It didn't matter how many sins she had committed, the blood was greater and more powerful than any sin.

Did you know that the blood of Jesus cries out for God's mercy, not His judgment? You may have ungodly neighbors, but they live next to you for a reason. Don't pray for God to give them judgment, pray that they will receive Jesus as Savior and Lord. The book of Proverbs states that your neighbors are safely protected when you keep them hedged in by the blood of Jesus: "Do not devise evil against your neighbor, for he dwells by you for safety's sake" (Proverbs 3:29). When your faith is in the blood of Jesus, it will not only provide protection for your household, but also for those around you.

The Lord provides shelter from every storm. He doesn't leave you out in the heat, but provides a shade that will supernaturally protect you.

CHAPTER 6

YAHWEH IS SALVATION

Have you ever been in charge of a group of people? Maybe you taught a class or led a ministry team or unit of coworkers in a specific task. When you were the leader, the responsibility was on you to lead. Regardless of what task you may be called on to lead others to accomplish, you have to be equipped, enabled, and empowered to lead effectively. This is what the grace of God does in you, through you, and for you. Jesus makes you who you are. He will equip, enable, and empower you. Joshua, a great man of God whose story we find in the Old Testament, understood this important principle. He learned to depend on the Lord and was successful in leading an entire nomadic nation into foreign territory to take it over as their own land.

I Will Never Leave You nor Forsake You

The successor to Moses and leader of the Israelite invasion of Canaan was *Hoshea* from the tribe of Ephraim, whose name means "salvation." His name was later changed by Moses to "Joshua" (Numbers 13:16), which means "Yahweh is salvation."[11] The

Lord (known as Yahweh) gave Joshua the key to becoming a successful leader – he was to make the Word of God his daily meditation.

> *This Book of the Law shall not depart from your mouth, but you shall meditate in it day and night, that you may observe to do according to all that is written in it. For then you will make your way prosperous, and then you will have good success.*

Joshua 1:8

When you keep the Word of God first place in your life, you become untouchable. God's Word in front of your eyes, in your ears, and coming out of your mouth takes root in your heart and produces faith. When he kept the Word of God first place in his mouth, mind, and heart, Joshua's enemies were not able to touch him: "No man shall be able to stand before you all the days of your life" (Joshua 1:5). Joshua was confident that no nation would be able to stand against the nation of Israel. He meditated day and night on the Torah and believed that the Lord was always with him: "As I was with Moses, so I will be with you. I will not leave you nor forsake you" (Joshua 1:5).

Joshua was commanded three times to be strong and of good courage (Joshua 1:6, 1:7, 1:9). When you know that the Lord is with you and will never leave you nor forsake you, you can be strong and of good courage, just like Joshua. The writer of Hebrews reminds us of this precious truth. Read this verse several times aloud; meditate on it and you will sense the strength and courage of the Lord rising up in your spirit.

> *For He [God] Himself has said, I will not in any way fail you nor give you up nor leave you without support. [I will] not, [I will] not, [I will] not in any degree leave you helpless nor forsake nor let [you] down (relax My hold on you)! [Assuredly not!]*

Hebrews 13:5, AMPC

When you believe and meditate on this promise that your Father God will never, never, never leave you nor forsake you, it will cause you to become strong and courageous. Your faith will grow stronger. You will know God has given you the land flowing with milk, honey, and…giants. But you don't have to worry about the giants since the Lord is with you and will not forsake you! Knowing that the Lord is with you will make you a giant slayer: "The LORD your God is giving you rest and is giving you this land" (Joshua 1:13).

The Lord Is with Us

Joshua recognized that the people of Canaan were without supernatural protection since the Lord was not with them. The Canaanites may have had some giants in their land, but they were a people without a blood covenant. Joshua believed this gave Israel the advantage. The giants of Canaan were about to become giant-sized pieces of bread to feed the wild animals.

David knew the story of Joshua and the Israelites, how Joshua had commanded the people to not fear the giants in the land: "Only do not rebel against the LORD, nor fear the people of the land, for they are our bread; their protection has departed from them, and the LORD is with us. Do not fear them" (Numbers 14:9). David drew on this knowledge when he recognized that Goliath was without a blood covenant. He called him an "uncircumcised Philistine" and boldly challenged him in the field of battle (1 Samuel 17:26).

When you have a revelation understanding of the blood covenant you have with your Father, it will make you strong and courageous against any giant-sized adversary. When you know that your Father is with you wherever you go and that He will never, never, never leave you nor forsake you, all fear and discouragement will fade away. You are in blood covenant together with the Almighty! This is all that matters.

This Day

While Israel was wandering in the desert, they failed to circumcise their sons born during that time. God instructed Joshua to have the second generation circumcised to show they were in blood covenant with Him: "At that time the LORD said to Joshua, 'Make flint knives for yourself, and circumcise the sons of Israel again the second time'" (Joshua 5:2).

After Joshua obeyed in the act of blood covenant, the Lord declared, "This day I have rolled away the reproach of Egypt from you" (Joshua 5:9). The day Israel honored the blood covenant by having their sons circumcised and taking Passover, the Lord rolled away the reproach of Egypt from them. Israel called the place "Gilgal," which means "rolling," because it was at that place – on that day – when God rolled away their reproach.

> *Then Joshua circumcised their sons whom He raised up in their place; for they were uncircumcised, because they had not been circumcised on the way... Then the LORD said to Joshua, "This day I have rolled away the reproach of Egypt from you." Therefore the name of the place is called Gilgal to this day. Now the children of Israel camped in Gilgal, and kept the Passover.*

> Joshua 5:7, 9-10

All of the devil's accusations, guilt, shame, and reproach that he has heaped on you are rolled away *This Day* - the day you honor the blood of Jesus. When you make the decision to cover yourself and your family with the blood of Jesus, *This Day* your reproach will be rolled away. Regardless of how many threats the devil has hurled at you, that day is over. *This Day* is the day the Lord has made and all the lies of the accuser have been flushed away. *This Day*, you and your family stand under the blood of Jesus in the secret place of the Most High. *This Day*, His blood has rolled away the curse from you and your family, as far as the East is from the West. Every day you honor the blood covenant becomes *This Day*. "This is the day the LORD has made, we will rejoice and be glad in it. Save now, I pray, send now prosperity" (Psalm 118:24-25).

It was after Israel honored the Lord in the blood covenant of circumcision and keeping the Passover that Joshua had a heavenly encounter. He lifted up his eyes and saw the Commander of the army of the Lord (Joshua 5:13). "Joshua went to Him and said to Him, 'Are You for us or for our adversaries?' So He said, 'No, but as Commander of the army of the LORD I have now come'" (Joshua 5:13-14). Notice that the Commander of the army of the Lord came the day Israel honored their blood covenant with Almighty God – *This Day*. When you honor the blood of Jesus, the blood of Jesus will honor you.

Isaiah - Yahweh Is Salvation

The name Isaiah has the same meaning as the name Joshua, "Yahweh is salvation."[12]   The prophet Isaiah is noted more for what he said than what he did, but Isaiah is recorded to have done some very unusual acts when prompted by the Lord. The Lord instructed Isaiah to walk the streets of Judah naked and without sandals for three years as a sign of divine judgment on Egypt and Ethiopia (Isaiah 20:2-4). Aren't you glad you were never given that spiritual assignment?! I doubt if Isaiah's friends and relatives ever invited him over for dinner during that season. Yet he was obedient, even at the cost of his own humiliation and discomfort.

Isaiah prophesied against Jerusalem and warned them that God had removed His divine protection from Judah, which would lead to their eventual captivity in Babylon (Isaiah 22:1-8). Isaiah warned Jerusalem that because they looked to their own armor as their defense and did not look to the Lord as their source of protection, they would be defenseless against their enemies.

> *He removed the protection of Judah. You looked in that day to the armor of the House of the Forest; you also saw the damage to the city of David, that it was great; and you gathered together the waters of the lower pool. You*

*numbered the houses of Jerusalem, and the houses you
broke down to fortify the wall. You also made a reservoir
between the two walls for the water of the old pool. But you
did not look to its Maker, nor did you have respect for Him
who fashioned it long ago.*

Isaiah 22:8-11

As they prepared for siege, Isaiah foresaw Jerusalem's defeat.
All of their efforts to protect themselves were in vain because the
inhabitants of Jerusalem were placing their trust in their own
strength and provision; they were not trusting in the Lord for their
salvation. Isaiah warned Judah that because their trust was in their
own efforts, the Lord's protection had been removed and they
would be defenseless against their enemies.

No matter how hard you strive to keep yourself and your family
safe, it will never suffice. Only when you make the Lord your
refuge and shelter do you not labor in vain. "Unless the LORD
builds the house, they labor in vain who build it; unless the LORD
guards the city, the watchman stays awake in vain" (Psalm 127:1).

The Shade of the Almighty

The twenty-fifth chapter of Isaiah declares praises for the
Lord's protection. In this passage, those who have made the Lord
their place of refuge are praising God for judging their enemies
and sheltering them from the attacks of the cruel and ruthless. The
poor and helpless are protected when they make the Lord their
place of shelter.

*For You have been a strength to the poor, a strength to the
needy in his distress, a refuge from the storm, a shade from
the heat; for the blast of the terrible ones is as a storm
against the wall.*

Isaiah 25:4

Notice that this verse says the Lord is, "a refuge from the storm, a shade from the heat; for the blast of the terrible ones is as a storm against the wall" (Isaiah 25:4). I live in South Florida where we celebrate the cool weather when it's 75 degrees. When I am outside on a very hot day, I always look for shade. When I take a walk, I always look for the side of the street that has the most shade. When I feel a breeze blow and I am standing under a shade tree, it feels so refreshing. That is a picture of standing underneath the shade of the Almighty.

Isaiah gives praise for the Lord for providing shade from the heat. He praises Him for being a place of supernatural protection. Isaiah praises the Lord for His salvation and for providing refuge to the poor, protection for the helpless and needy, and for being a fortress to run to during times of danger. When you feel the heat of an attack, you have a place to hide. The Lord provides shelter from every storm. He doesn't leave you out in the heat, but provides a shade that will supernaturally protect you.

> *You will reduce the noise of aliens, as heat in a dry place; as heat in the shadow of a cloud, the song of the terrible ones will be diminished.*

Isaiah 25:5

Kept in Shalom Shalom

Isaiah continues praising the Lord for His supernatural protection in chapter twenty-six.

> *In that day this song will be sung in the land of Judah: "We have a strong city; God will appoint salvation for walls and bulwarks. Open the gates, that the righteous nation which keeps the truth may enter in. You will keep him in perfect peace, whose mind is stayed on You, because he trusts in You. Trust in the LORD forever, For in YAH, the LORD, is everlasting strength.*

Isaiah 26:1-4

Those who trust in the Lord's protection experience true and complete peace, even when facing great tribulation: "You will keep him in perfect peace, whose mind is stayed on You, because he trusts in You" (Isaiah 26:3). The two words translated "perfect peace" in verse three are both the same Hebrew word, shalom.[13] In the original language, this verse would read "You will keep him in shalom, shalom." Perfect peace - shalom, shalom - is not derived from outside circumstances but is a divine blessing of the Lord. The Apostle Paul called it "the peace of God" (Philippians 4:6-7).

Do you have peace when your teenager gets behind the wheel of your car? If not, then you are probably not taking advantage of the blood covenant. When you trust in the Lord as your salvation and protection, you will witness a divine blessing of the Lord's peace as you always put your trust in Him.

Every time our kids go anywhere, we have them covered with the blood. It doesn't matter if they are just going to visit a friend down the street or going outside to ride a skateboard, Lena and I cover them with the blood of Jesus and pronounce the Lord's protection on them. When you do this as a lifestyle, it becomes second nature. It's not burdensome, mechanical, mystical or religious. Dwelling in the secret place allows you to enter into rest and experience the peace of God. When you trust in the Lord's protection and keep your mind stayed on Him, you will experience shalom shalom - His perfect peace.

CHAPTER 7

 og

WATCHMEN ON YOUR WALLS

Have you ever really meditated on the fact that angels are
with you wherever you go, to keep you protected? You may not
have noticed, but there are probably hundreds of thousands of
times the angels of God have provided protection for you and your
family. You may have never seen an angel, but they are present.
The world of entertainment portrays angels as weak little infants or
beautiful women and portrays demons as having great powers.
The truth is that we have the supernatural power and the devil has
nothing but lies and deception. What you are about to see in the
scripture is a picture of what one angel of the Lord can do to the
enemies of God's people.

Isaiah prophesied the Assyrian invasion of Jerusalem would be
a failure and that the Lord would protect Judah:

> *Therefore thus says the LORD concerning the king of
> Assyria: "He shall not come into this city, nor shoot an
> arrow there, nor come before it with shield, nor build a
> siege mound against it. By the way that he came, by the
> same shall he return; and he shall not come into this city,"*

67

says the LORD. "For I will defend this city, to save it for My own sake and for My servant David's sake."

Isaiah 37:33-35

When King Hezekiah of Judah heard the threats of the Assyrian king, he went to the house of the Lord and prayed for deliverance and protection. The Assyrians had laid to waste all other nations, but the King of Judah was trusting in the Lord's divine protection (Isaiah 37:15-20). In response to King Hezekiah's prayer, the angel of the Lord went out and slew one hundred and eighty-five thousands Assyrian troops in one day (Isaiah 37:36). God defended Jerusalem from the Assyrian armies using only one angelic host.

Think about how one angel wiped out an entire army. One angel of God is able to defend an entire city. This is an example of the miraculous power of the angelic hosts of heaven! One angel shut the mouths of lions (Daniel 6:16-23). One angel saved the three Hebrew men in the fiery furnace (Daniel 3:24-28). One angel saved Paul and an entire crew from being shipwrecked in a fatal storm (Acts 27:22-25). Rest in the fact that the angel of the Lord is watching over you when you dwell in the secret place.

When you make the Lord your dwelling place, the host of heaven will keep you in all your ways (Psalm 91:11-12). This is why Moses knew that Israel had nothing to fear when facing the army of Egypt at the Red Sea: "Do not be afraid. Stand still and see the salvation of the LORD…The LORD will fight for you, and you shall hold your peace… And the Angel of God, who went before the camp of Israel, moved and went behind them" (Exodus 14:13-14, 19). Only one angel fought the Egyptians at the Red Sea. One angel took on the entire army of Egypt! The promise in Psalm 91 is that when you dwell in the secret place, the Lord's angels (plural) shall keep you in all your ways (Psalm 91:11-12). If one angel can take on an entire army, how much more can angels keep you safe as you go about your life's business? You have nothing to fear when you know the angels of heaven go before you: "Behold, I send an Angel before you to keep you in the way" (Exodus 23:20).

Transported by Angels

When Lena was around 10 years old, she lived in Westchester, New York. One time, Lena was riding her bicycle with her cousin and was going down a steep hill in the middle of the road. Her cousin went down the hill first and saw a car coming. She screamed, "Lena, watch out! A car is coming!" Lena saw the car in front of her face about to hit her when all of a sudden, she found herself sitting on the side of the road in the grass with her bicycle lying next to her. She couldn't figure out how she went from being in the middle of the road about to be run over, to suddenly sitting in the grass - all in a split second. It was years later after she'd learned about angels that she understood what had happened. She had been afforded supernatural protection.

There are accounts throughout the Bible of God's people being transported by angels or by the Spirit of God. The angels supernaturally transported Philip to Azotus, which was twenty miles north of Gaza (Acts 8:38-40). Obadiah spoke of how Elijah was transported by the Spirit of God: "And it shall come to pass, as soon as I am gone from you, that the Spirit of the LORD will carry you to a place I do not know" (1 Kings 18:12). The sons of the prophets also talked of how the Spirit of the Lord would transport Elijah to another location supernaturally: "Perhaps the Spirit of the LORD has taken him up and cast him upon some mountain or into some valley" (2 Kings 2:16).

Lena was safely transported from the middle of the road to sitting on the side of the road through angelic conveyance. When you declare that the Lord is your refuge, He will send His angel before you to keep you in all your ways.

Declare Salvation upon Your Walls

Does it seem like you are living in times of great darkness? The world seems to be getting darker and deeper into sin. The good news is that the Church is getting brighter and deeper into the light of God's Word. We may be living in dark times, but the light of the glory of the Lord has risen upon us.

Isaiah 60 extends the blood covenant of protection to the Gentiles who have seen the light of God's glory: "Arise, shine; for your light has come! And the glory of the LORD is risen upon you. For behold, the darkness shall cover the earth, and deep darkness the people; but the LORD will arise over you, and His glory will be seen upon you. The Gentiles shall come to your light, and kings to the brightness of your rising" (Isaiah 60:1-3).

The Lord assures us that in these days of darkness, the world will see His glory upon us. Even the rulers of nations will see the glory of God on the Body of Christ. The world is going to witness the supernatural protection of the Lord during these dark and violent times. You have authority through the blood covenant to declare that violence shall no longer be heard in your neighborhood. The reason violence shall no longer be heard in your land is because you have declared "Salvation" upon your walls: "Violence shall no longer be heard in your land, neither wasting nor destruction within your borders; but you shall call your walls Salvation, and your gates Praise" (Isaiah 60:18).

This declaration of Salvation over your walls and borders is simply exercising faith in the blood covenant of protection. Remember that the name Jesus means, "Yahweh is salvation." When you declare Jesus is Lord over your land, you are declaring Salvation upon the walls of your city, your neighborhood, your community, your subdivision, your apartment community, your nation.

Watchmen on Your Walls

I'm sure if you look back at your life, you can recall times when the Lord provided His supernatural protection, even if you were not aware that someone was praying divine protection over you. When I was a little boy, I nearly drowned in a pool in Houston, Texas. I almost choked to death twice. In my early years of driving, I was in five major car accidents. Three of those incidents were my own dumb fault for reckless driving. In one accident, I was a passenger. And in the fifth accident, I was hit by a drunk driver. In all five incidents, I was saved when I could have been seriously injured or even killed.

I remember in one of those accidents, I was sitting in the passenger's seat. My head smashed the car windshield, busted the dashboard, and broke the passenger window. The driver of the car said my head looked like it was going off in a pinball machine. Later that evening, I was released from the hospital without any serious injuries. There was always someone – parents, a family member, a pastor, church family - who was praying God's supernatural protection over me. Thank the Lord for watchmen who know how to pray!

I'm sure you can think of times when you could have been killed but you were saved supernaturally. In your early years, you may have had watchmen praying over you. It may have been a parent, relative, church member, pastor, or neighbor. You may not even have been aware, but they covered you in divine protection. These watchmen were sent by God.

I have set watchmen on your walls, O Jerusalem; they shall never hold their peace day or night. You who make mention of the LORD, do not keep silent.

Isaiah 62:6

A watchman does not keep silent, but keeps the entire family covered with prayers day and night. The watchman stays alert, making sure the walls of protection provided by the blood of Jesus surround family, friends, church members, community, and city. You may be the only watchman in your family. Others may be depending on your intercessory prayers. It would be good for you to let them know that they are in your prayers. This will help them recognize God's supernatural protection when they encounter danger.

You may wake up in the middle of the night and sense in your heart that you need to pray over a police officer, a neighbor, a church member, or someone in your family. It is vital for you to be spiritually alert as you take the call of a watchman. "But the end of all things is at hand; therefore be serious and watchful in your prayers" (1 Peter 4:7).

Hanging on the Side of Clingman's Dome

My wife, like her grandmother, is a watchman and is always watchful to intercede for others. One time, Lena and her grandmother were both awakened in the middle of the night with an urgency to pray for divine protection over Lena's sister and her husband. They both sensed that the couple was in danger of being in a serious car accident, so they prayed for God's divine protection. The next morning, Lena's sister felt an urgency to cover herself, her husband and their rented car with the blood of Jesus. Later that very afternoon, they would experience an amazing miracle of supernatural protection.

While on vacation, Lena's sister and her husband were on Clingman's Dome, the highest peak in the Smokey Mountains. They decided to drive up to the top of the mountain to view the magnificent scenery and when they reached the peak, Lena's brother-in-law pulled over to carefully park the car along the side of the road. The problem was, the road near the top of the mountain is very narrow and there is an immediate drop off down the side of a cliff. The car started to slide off the side of the road and down the cliff. Lena's sister and brother-in-law were trapped inside the car at the very edge of the cliff. Just before the car went airborne, it suddenly stopped moving and was hanging at the edge. As they sat in the car looking down at a 6,000 foot drop, they did not want to move, afraid the slightest movement might send the car over the edge.

From the road, no one could see their car as it hung off the side of the mountain. Eventually, Lena's brother-in-law was able to pull his wife out of the car and they were able to climb to safety. It took two tow trucks to pull the rented car up off the side of Clingman's Dome. They later found that the car was being held in place by only two little shrubs. Lena's sister and her husband would call those shrubs "the hands of God."

Now imagine for a moment if Lena, her grandmother, and her sister had not prayed for the Lord's divine protection. What would have happened? What if Lena had simply shrugged off the unction to pray and went back to sleep? What would have happened if Lena's grandmother had stayed up all night worrying, but failed to pray? What would have happened if Lena's sister was too busy to cover herself, her husband, and their rented car with the blood of Jesus? The answer is simple: premature death. It is not the will of God for any of us to die prematurely. This is why the calling of a watchman is so vitally important.

A watchman is on duty 24/7, all day and all night, alert for the promptings, unction, and warnings of the Holy Spirit. The Lord may wake you up in the middle of the night and you'll have the urgency to pray for someone. The reason you are thinking about that person is because God is using you to be His watchman.

The Lord is not calling you to be His watchman because you hold a title in a local church. He is not calling you based on how many scriptures you have memorized. He is not looking to you because of your motivational or leadership abilities. He simply needs someone who is available to pray, believe, and exercise dominion. That person is…YOU!

Someone may be in serious trouble and the Lord is depending on you to be the watchman! Don't be surprised if before you finish reading this book, you begin to have promptings to pray for someone in your family, a friend, a neighbor, or an acquaintance. When you pass a car accident on the side of the highway, take time to cover those involved with the blood. If you see a careless driver or a motorcyclist fly past you, don't shout abusive words at them. No! Be a watchman and cover them with divine protection. The mercy of the Lord is everlasting and available to all. Your neighbor may know nothing about the power of the blood, but they dwell next to you for safety's sake (Proverbs 3:29). Their life may depend on you keeping a hedge of protection around them.

CHAPTER 8

NO WEAPON

"No weapon formed against you shall prosper, and every tongue which rises against you in judgment you shall condemn. This is the heritage of the servants of the LORD, and their righteousness is from Me," says the LORD.

Isaiah 54:17

Covenant of Peace: Isaiah 54

In the book of Isaiah, there are four "Servant Songs" that speak of the coming of Messiah. Out of the four songs, Isaiah 52:13-53:12 is the most well-known. The fourth "Servant Song" speaks of the suffering of Messiah and the triumphant Church. In this passage, Messiah takes the penalty and curse of sin and makes available to everyone redemption and forgiveness. The promise of peace, protection, and well-being are included in this passage: "The chastisement for our peace was upon Him" (Isaiah 53:5). Messiah was to take our punishment so that we may have shalom.

Jesus suffered our punishment to provide for our safety and well-being.

> *Surely our diseases he did bear, and our pains he carried; whereas we did esteem him stricken, smitten of God, and afflicted. But he was wounded because of our transgressions, he was crushed because of our iniquities: the chastisement of our welfare was upon him, and with his stripes we were healed.*

> Isaiah 53:4-5, THS

The sacrifice of the Servant provides redemption to all those who will receive it by faith. Isaiah 54 then speaks of the Lord's blood covenant of protection that is provided for those who are redeemed.

Covenant of Shalom

You have been given a covenant of peace with the Almighty. His arm has been revealed, the good report of His covenant of peace is for you to believe and receive. His covenant of peace and completeness (shalom) will never fail, even if everything around you is shaken and collapsing.

> *"For the mountains shall depart and the hills be removed, but My kindness shall not depart from you, nor shall My covenant of peace be removed," says the LORD, who has mercy on you.*

> Isaiah 54:10

You have been given a covenant of shalom with the Lord who assures your complete safety, welfare, and quietness in the midst of destruction. In the midst of a chaotic world, you can experience shalom externally because you have shalom internally.

The mountains may disappear [move; be shaken], and the hills may come to an end [be removed; disappear], but my love [lovingkindness; loyalty; covenant love] will never disappear [be moved/shaken]; my promise [covenant; treaty] of peace will not come to an end [be removed; disappear]," says the LORD who shows mercy to [has compassion for] you.

Isaiah 54:10, EXB

The Lord's promise of peace and protection will never come to an end or be removed from you. You have a covenant of shalom with the Father that will never disappear, be removed, or shaken. His covenant love for you will never come to an end. It is forever!

Shalom on Your Children

My wife and I have ministered with teenagers for over twenty years. We have always had a connection with youth. They are not only the church of the future, but they are a vital part of the church of today.

No generation before has been like this one. No generation has had such access to the world's wide web of entanglements and distractions, never before has there been such infiltration into the minds of our youth and children. Satan has attempted to lure and addict this generation with pride, lust, fame, and the pleasures of this world. The devil is scared of the potential contained in the youth of these last days. He is afraid of the young millennial believers who dwell in the secret place and know their dominion. He is afraid of the prophecy of Joel coming to pass, where the young men and young women cover this planet with the gospel of Christ (Joel 2:28-32). Your children, both natural and spiritual, must be trained in the understanding of their blood covenant (Proverbs 22:6). You must keep them covered in the blood and safe underneath the shadow of the Almighty.

Lena and I have seen teenagers delivered from every kind of evil, including sex trafficking. One youth who had just received Christ was kidnapped. We covered her in the blood of Jesus and let the devil know he had picked the wrong girl! We told the devil that she was under our spiritual authority and we covered her with the blood of Jesus. We believed that no weapon formed against her would prosper, in Jesus' name. Within a few days, this girl was rescued and testified of the Lord's supernatural protection.

We have seen other teenagers and children healed from chronic diseases, delivered from addiction and suicide, set free from fear, and filled with the Father's love, joy, and peace. Over the many years, we have watched these children and teens grow up and become mighty "blood warriors" for Christ.

The Lord is comforting the storm-tossed children and teens of this world. He is setting His glory and brilliance upon the children and youth of today: "O you afflicted one, tossed with tempest, and not comforted...All your children shall be taught by the Lord, and great shall be the peace of your children" (Isaiah 54:11, 13).

You and your children should not have to live in this world afflicted, storm-tossed and in fear and depression. You have been redeemed and given a covenant of shalom for your family. Your children are to be taught by the Lord and experience His great peace and undisturbed composure.

Far from the Thought of Destruction

In this tremendous covenant of shalom, you will experience God's divine peace and will have undisturbed composure. You will no longer be afflicted and storm-tossed. You will know what it's like to have shalom on your home. When you refuse to fear, terror cannot come near you or your dwelling.

> *In righteousness you shall be established; you shall be far from oppression, for you shall not fear; and from terror, for it shall not come near you.*

Isaiah 54:14

What used to upset you will no longer enter your mind. The fear of terror that used to oppress you will not be able to come near you. This is what happens when you believe, receive, and act on the blood covenant of shalom.

The Lord promises that those who rise up against you will fall in surrender: "Indeed they shall surely assemble, but not because of Me. Whoever assembles against you shall fall for your sake" (Isaiah 54:15). The devil has no answer when you come against him with the blood of Jesus. Your Father makes it clear that He does not send the devastator to destroy and stir up strife. Jesus informed His disciples that He came to save and not destroy: "For the Son of Man did not come to destroy men's lives but to save them" (Luke 9:56). Father God sent Jesus, not to destroy the lives of men, but to destroy the works of the enemy: "For this purpose the Son of God was manifested, that He might destroy the works of the devil" (1 John 3:8).

The heritage of the Lord's servant is divine protection from every weapon of the enemy. This is not just limited to weapons such as guns, knives, and swords, but includes every carnal weapon, emotional weapon, and spiritual weapon the enemy has ever used including death itself. The Lord provides protection from storms, catastrophes, accidents, diseases, viruses, terrorism, poisoning, bullying, abuse, fear, regret, depression, oppression, and any other weapon the devil has used to steal, kill, and destroy.

"You Cannot Kill Me!"

Dr. Terry Mize, a world missionary and apostle for over forty years, tells of how the Lord supernaturally protected him while in Mexico. He had just picked up a hitchhiker when suddenly, the man pulled out a gun and threatened to kill him. Terry stated that the hitchhiker shoved the gun into his ribs and screamed, "I'm going to kill you!" Terry told the man, "You cannot kill me! I have authority over you, in the name of Jesus. You cannot harm me in any way." The hitchhiker continued to threaten to kill him and each time Terry would tell him, "I have authority over you, in the name of Jesus." Terry kept God's Word inside his heart and mouth and refused to fear. He reminded the Lord what His blood covenant declares:

All authority has been given to Me in heaven and on earth.

Matthew 28:18

Behold, I give you authority to trample on serpents and scorpions, and over all the power of the enemy, and nothing shall by any means hurt you.

Luke 10:19

Terry kept saying over and over, "Jesus said that I have authority over all the power of the enemy and nothing shall by any means hurt me!" Terry was releasing words of faith in the blood covenant, which put the ministering spirits to work. When the man asked Terry if he was afraid, he answered "Why should I be afraid? All you have is a loaded gun, but I have the name of Jesus."[14]

The hitchhiker told Terry to pull over and got out of the car, taking the keys to the car with him. Terry testified that at that moment, he stuck his finger in the face of the hitchhiker and told him, "I rebuke you in the name of Jesus Christ of Nazareth! You cannot kill me or hurt me in any way!" The hitchhiker was now furious. He pointed the gun straight at Terry and shot at point blank range five times. All five bullets fell to the ground between Terry's feet.[15] What blocked the bullets? Terry was dwelling in the secret place. Terry's faith was not in his own strength or ability but in the power of the name of Jesus, the blood, and the Word of God. Terry invited the man to his house and said he would help him out in any way. He also commanded the man to give back his keys, "I have authority in this situation. Now, give me back my keys in Jesus' name!"[16] The hitchhiker handed back the keys, Terry's watch and wedding ring and gave his heart to Jesus as Lord and savior.

Even with a gun pointed at his face, Terry refused to fear and remained safe inside the hedge of protection: "You shall not be afraid of the terror by night, nor of the arrow that flies by day" (Psalm 91:5). You may have a feeling of fear but not have the spirit of fear in your heart. The way to know what is in your heart is by hearing what comes out of your mouth.

Out of the Abundance of the Heart

When faith is in your heart, God's Word will come out of your mouth. When fear is in your heart, then fear will come out of your mouth. Prior to this incident, Dr. Terry had been listening to the Word of God in his car. When he picked up the hitchhiker, he already had faith in his heart. Jesus stated that whatever is in your heart, good or bad, will eventually come out of your mouth and tell on you.

> *A good man out of the good treasure of his heart brings forth good; and an evil man out of the evil treasure of his heart brings forth evil. For out of the abundance of the heart his mouth speaks.*

Luke 6:45

If fear comes out of your mouth, then what has been stored up in your heart is fear. When faith comes out of your mouth in times of danger, it shows that God's Word has been stored up in your heart. If wrong words have been coming out of your mouth, then repent right now. Don't delay another second. "Lord, I repent and receive Your forgiveness of speaking wrong words." Make the quality decision to feed your faith with God's Word and starve fear to death.

How Do You Plead?

When you are in blood covenant with the Lord, dwelling in His secret place, you are promised that no weapon of the enemy will succeed. You have received the Lord's righteousness and are justified by faith in Jesus Christ. His blood has made you righteous and blameless as if you never sinned. When the accuser comes against you, the blood of Jesus will protect you.

> *"No weapon formed against you shall prosper, and every tongue which rises against you in judgment you shall condemn. This is the heritage of the servants of the LORD, and their righteousness is from Me," says the LORD.*

Isaiah 54:17

Every time the enemy's tongue rises up against you in judgment, accusing you of past sins, you should always respond with the blood. The devil cries, "You are guilty! You deserve death!" How should you respond? How do you plead? Don't plead, "Yes, I'm guilty. I'm just an unworthy worm who's been saved by grace." You should always respond, "I am the righteousness of God in Christ Jesus and I plead the blood!" Say aloud right now, "I am the righteousness of God in Christ and I plead the blood of Jesus. No weapon formed against me shall prosper!"

When you come against the accuser with your own unworthiness, his weapons will prosper against you. But when you stand against the accuser in the righteousness of God in Christ Jesus, the accusations fall to the ground. Faith in the blood of Jesus always wins in the courts of Heaven. The accuser hates the blood. He will stomp out of the courtroom screaming, "This trial isn't fair! You're ignoring all the evidence!" Your faith in the blood overrides all the devil's accusations. The blood always wins!

Every time you stand against the devil's accusations with the blood of Jesus, you overcome him: "For the accuser of our brethren, he who keeps bringing before our God charges against them day and night, has been cast out! And they have overcome (conquered) him by means of the blood of the Lamb and by the utterance of their testimony" (Revelation 12:10-11, AMPC).

When the devil rises up with his accusations and declares, "You are guilty," you overcome him with your testimony by declaring, "The blood of the Lamb has made me innocent!" There is nothing the accuser can use against you when you plead the blood of the Lamb as your testimony. Say this with me, "The blood of the Lamb has made me innocent, blameless, spotless, justified, cleansed, and forgiven. No weapon formed against me shall prosper, for I am the righteousness of God in Christ Jesus!"

The choice of life and death is not in the hands of God. He has given you the choice of life or death, blessing or curses.

CHAPTER 9

C>

REDEEMED FROM DEATH
AND DESTRUCTION

Bless the LORD, O my soul; and all that is within me, bless
His holy name! Bless the LORD, O my soul, and forget not
all His benefits; who forgives all your iniquities, who heals
all your diseases, who redeems your life from destruction,
who crowns you with lovingkindness and tender mercies,
who satisfies your mouth with good things so that your
youth is renewed like the eagle's.

Psalm 103:1-5

In Psalm 103, David declares how the Lord redeemed his life
from destruction. David blesses the Lord for His lovingkindness,
His tender mercies, and for satisfying his life with good things.
David understood that it was the Lord who redeemed his life from
destruction and premature death.

After Samuel anointed David as the king of Israel to replace Saul, David was chosen by Saul to become his armor bearer (1 Samuel 16:21). When David heard of the threats and insults made against Israel by the Philistine champion warrior Goliath, he told Saul, "Your servant has killed both lion and bear; and this uncircumcised Philistine will be like one of them, seeing he has defied the armies of the living God" (1 Samuel 17:36). David knew it was the Lord who had redeemed his life from death and destruction.

Notice that David never called Goliath a giant. He called Goliath an "uncircumcised Philistine." Didn't David notice that the height of Goliath was well over nine feet, nine inches tall (1 Samuel 17:4)? Wasn't David able to see that his opponent was wearing armor weighing over 125 pounds (1 Samuel 17:5) and that the head of his spear weighed over 15 pounds (1 Samuel 17:7)? Was David denying the fact that he was facing a giant of a man?

David was not in denial. He was not blinded by false hope. David just refused to allow his heart to be filled with fear. He would not be swayed by Goliath's stature and strength: "Let no man's heart fail because of him" (1 Samuel 17:32). David did not consider his own small stature, his inexperience, his youthful weakness, or his homemade weapon. He knew that the Lord had redeemed his life from death and destruction. He believed that the Almighty would deliver him again, "Moreover David said, 'The LORD, who delivered me from the paw of the lion and from the paw of the bear, He will deliver me from the hand of this Philistine'" (1 Samuel 17:37).

David's attention was focused on one thing only – *I am circumcised and Goliath is uncircumcised. I am in blood covenant with God Almighty and Goliath is not.* David went toe to toe with Goliath acting as one who had the advantage, not as the underdog or as a weak shepherd boy.

The great heavyweight boxer Muhammad Ali used to tell his opponents, "I'm gonna knock you out," and he would tell them in what round he intended to do it. He did this before the match ever started. Even when he faced some fierce opponents, Ali would speak the desired end result. This is a spiritual law of faith that works when you work it. David declared himself the champion before the fight began. David informed Goliath what would be the outcome of the match: "This day the LORD will deliver you into my hand, and I will strike you and take your head from you...Then all this assembly shall know that the LORD does not save with sword and spear; for the battle is the LORD's, and He will give you into our hands" (1 Samuel 17:46-47).

David did not rely on his weapon, but relied on his blood covenant with the Lord. He knew it was the Lord who would cause him to triumph over Goliath: "So David prevailed over the Philistine with a sling and a stone, and struck the Philistine and killed him. But there was no sword in the hand of David" (1 Samuel 17:50).

Redeemed from the Curse

I'll never forget the time I was asked by a witch to pray for his sick dog. At the time, I was a young minister serving in a local church as youth pastor. One afternoon, there was a knock on the church door. I opened it up to find a strangely dressed young man and his dog. The young man introduced himself as a witch and requested that I pray for his dog to be healed. He shared with me, "I was told by my parents, who are both witches, that you have white magic powers." The young man's parents had visited the church several times and always left sitting on their chair a bag filled with glitter, symbolic writings, and other eccentric things. I had found their bag a number of times and wondered what all that stuff was about.

I explained to the young man that I did not have any magical powers, but agreed to pray for his dog on one condition - that he would allow me to pray for him first. He agreed and I laid hands on his chest, rebuked the evil spirits out of him in Jesus' name, and prayed with him to receive Jesus Christ as his Lord and Savior. When he asked me about curses that might later come upon him or his dog, I explained that the blood of Jesus cleanses him from every curse and evil spirit. "Jesus has made you a new creation," I told him. I had him say aloud with me, "I am forgiven, cleansed, blameless, justified, righteous, healed and delivered from every curse." I let him know no matter how much evil was in his background, the blood of Jesus had reversed every curse. I told him, "You are a new creation. You are blessed!"

When you are in Christ, you are redeemed from the curse: "Christ has redeemed us from the curse of the law, having become a curse for us (for it is written, 'Cursed is everyone who hangs on a tree') that the blessing of Abraham might come upon the Gentiles in Christ Jesus, that we might receive the promise of the Spirit through faith" (Galatians 3:13-14). This "blessing of Abraham" includes redemption from the curse of destruction and shortness of life.

> *Who redeems your life from destruction, who crowns you with lovingkindness and tender mercies, who satisfies your mouth with good things so that your youth is renewed like the eagle's.*
>
> Psalm 103:4-5

You are the redeemed of the Lord. Now it is up to you to say that it is so: "Let the redeemed of the LORD say so, whom He has redeemed from the hand of the enemy" (Psalm 107:2).

A Command to Bless

Under the leadership of Moses, Israel increased in numbers causing their enemies to fear them: "And Moab was exceedingly afraid of the people because they were many, and Moab was sick with dread because of the children of Israel" (Numbers 22:3).

The Moabite king, Balak, hired a Mesopotamian sorcerer, Balaam, whose name means "to swallow and to ruin."[17] In those days, sorcerers or magicians were used for pronouncing curses on people, rulers, or nations. Balak hired Balaam to curse Israel in exchange for a large reward (Numbers 22:6-7).

When Balak's men first approached Balaam requesting his services, God told Balaam, "You shall not go with them; you shall not curse the people, for they are blessed" (Numbers 22:12), so Balaam refused to return with Balak's men. When Balak was made aware of Balaam's refusal, that he would not curse Israel, he offered to raise the diviner's fee (Numbers 22:17); but Balaam replied he would not be able to change the blessing to a curse, even with the promise of a great reward: "Though Balak were to give me his house full of silver and gold, I could not go beyond the word of the LORD" (Numbers 22:18). Isn't that awesome! Though the demonized sorcerer tried his best to curse Israel, all he could do was pronounce the blessing. Under the Abrahamic covenant blessing, you are blessed and redeemed from the curse.

Eventually, Balaam accepted the king's offer after he had a vision in which God instructed him to follow Balak's men (Numbers 22:20). But when the enchanter journeyed out to curse Israel, the Angel of the Lord stood in his way: "And the Angel of the LORD took His stand in the way as an adversary against him" (Numbers 22:22). The donkey Balaam was riding saw the Angel of the Lord standing in the middle of the road with His sword drawn in His hand and stopped in his tracks. Balaam beat the donkey with his staff, unaware of why the donkey would not move forward. The donkey saw into the realm of the Spirit and lay down in fear of the Angel of the Lord (Numbers 22:27).

Balaam became so infuriated that he began arguing with the donkey (Numbers 22:29-30). You may have yelled at your dog before, but I'm sure it never yelled back (except to say "bow wow"). In this case, however, the donkey replied to Balaam. There is no sign that the sorcerer was afraid when the donkey replied to him. Balaam had a conversation with the donkey, as if this was a common occurrence. It is possible that prior to this event, Balaam the sorcerer had heard voices coming from animals possessed by demons.

So the donkey said to Balaam, "Am I not your donkey on which you have ridden, ever since I became yours, to this day? Was I ever disposed to do this to you?" And he said, "No."

Then the LORD opened Balaam's eyes, and he saw the Angel of the LORD standing in the way with His drawn sword in His hand; and he bowed his head and fell flat on his face. And the Angel of the LORD said to him, "Why have you struck your donkey these three times? Behold, I have come out to stand against you, because your way is perverse before Me. The donkey saw Me and turned aside from Me these three times. If she had not turned aside from Me, surely I would also have killed you by now, and let her live."

Numbers 22:30-33

Before departing, the Angel warned Balaam to speak only what God put in his mouth and nothing else (Numbers 22:35). When Balaam arrived in the area overlooking the Israelites, he declared the blessing over Israel and not a curse. The king of Moab was furious and asked, "What have you done to me? I took you to curse my enemies, and look, you have blessed them bountifully" (Numbers 23:11). The sorcerer replied, "Must I not take heed to speak what the LORD has put in my mouth?" (Numbers 23:12). Balaam had worshiped Baal of Peor, but even he recognized that the God of Israel is greater than the god of Baal.

Multiple times, this scene was repeated. Balak offered blood sacrifices and did everything he could to entice Balaam to curse Israel, but it was all to no avail. The blood covenant is greater than any pagan blood sacrifice. God had determined to bless Israel and they would be blessed. Did you know you are redeemed from the curse? Jesus has reversed the curse and the devil cannot reverse the blessing.

Balaam had been given a command to bless and he could not do otherwise. Israel was redeemed from the curses of divination because of the Lord's blood covenant of protection over them: "He has not observed iniquity in Jacob, nor has He seen wickedness in Israel...for there is no sorcery against Jacob, nor any divination against Israel. It now must be said of Jacob and of Israel, 'Oh, what God has done!'" (Numbers 23:21, 23).

When Balaam pronounced the blessing over Israel, he prophesied of the coming Messiah: "His king shall be higher than Agag, and his kingdom shall be exalted, God brings him out of Egypt; He has strength like a wild ox...Blessed is he who blesses you, and cursed is he who curses you....A Star shall come out of Jacob; a Scepter shall rise out of Israel and batter the brow of Moab" (Numbers 24:7-9, 17). God's Son, the Messiah, solidified for all time the blood covenant of protection.

At a later time, the Lord instructed Moses to take vengeance on the Midianites by sending out one thousand from each tribe of Israel into battle. All the men of Midian were killed, as well as Balaam the sorcerer (Numbers 31:8). The Apostle Peter referred to Balaam as a false prophet (2 Peter 2:15-16). The Apostle John referred to Balaam as the one who taught Balak to put an obstacle before the children of Israel (Revelation 2:14). The intentions of Balaam were clearly to pronounce a curse over Israel for the sake of profit, but ultimately, he was only able to speak the blessing.

THE BLESSING

And all these blessings shall come upon you and overtake you, because you obey the voice of the LORD your God.

Deuteronomy 28:2

Let's take a look at the blessing described in Deuteronomy 28. Notice that this blessing includes longevity of life, tranquility, and protection.

Blessed shall you be in the city, and blessed shall you be in the country.

Deuteronomy 28:3

Blessed shall you be when you come in, and blessed shall you be when you go out.

Deuteronomy 28:6

The LORD will cause your enemies who rise against you to be defeated before your face; they shall come out against you one way and flee before you seven ways.

Deuteronomy 28:7

He will bless you in the land which the LORD your God is giving you.

Deuteronomy 28:8

Then all peoples of the earth shall see that you are called by the name of the LORD, and they shall be afraid of you.

Deuteronomy 28:10

The curse, which is described in Deuteronomy 28:15-68, includes destruction, devastation, and shortness of life. When you read the curses listed in Deuteronomy 28:15-68, you should get just as excited as when you read the blessing listed in Deuteronomy 28:1-14, because Jesus has reversed the curse and has given you the blessing! For example, when you read the curse mentioned in Deuteronomy 28:66: "Your life shall hang in doubt before you; you shall fear day and night, and have no assurance of life," because of Jesus, you can now reverse the curse with the blessing: "I am redeemed from the curse and I am blessed, therefore, my life shall never hang in doubt and I shall not be afraid both day and night. The Lord has given me the assurance of long life!"

Here are some other examples:

The Curse

"You shall beget sons and daughters, but they shall not be yours; for they shall go into captivity" (Deuteronomy 28:41).

Reversed to the Blessing

"I am redeemed from the curse and I am blessed, therefore, my children shall be protected from being harmed, injured, or kidnapped. They shall never go into captivity."

The Curse

"The LORD will send on you cursing, confusion, and rebuke in all that you set your hand to do, until you are destroyed and until you perish quickly" (Deuteronomy 28:20).

Reversed to the Blessing

"I am redeemed from the curse and I am blessed, therefore, all that I set my hand to do is blessed. I and my entire family are redeemed from destruction and we shall enjoy long life."

The Curse

"Your ox shall be slaughtered before your eyes, but you shall not eat of it; your donkey shall be violently taken away from before you, and shall not be restored to you; your sheep shall be given to your enemies, and you shall have no one to rescue them" (Deuteronomy 28:31).

<u>Reversed to the Blessing</u>

"I am redeemed from the curse and I am blessed, therefore, my possessions and equipment shall not be destroyed nor shall it be taken away from me. Everything the devil has stolen in the past shall be rescued and restored back to me sevenfold" (Proverbs 6:31).

<u>The Curse</u>

"Moreover He will bring back on you all the diseases of Egypt, of which you were afraid, and they shall cling to you. Also every sickness and every plague, which is not written in this Book of the Law, will the LORD bring upon you until you are destroyed" (Deuteronomy 28:60-61).

<u>Reversed to the Blessing</u>

"I am redeemed from the curse and I am blessed, therefore, every disease, every sickness, and every plague that is under the curse shall not come near me. I am redeemed from every disease, every sickness, every virus, and every plague for the Lord is my redeemer."

Take some time to study Deuteronomy 28. Read aloud each verse and declare the blessing - and declare that the curse has been reversed!

Choose Life - Choose Blessing

My family enjoys watching movies together at home and eating popcorn. (My favorite snack is freshly popped popcorn - not microwaved – topped with butter, a little sea salt, honey, and a sprinkle of cinnamon. Delish!) Recently, we watched a Christian movie in which a pastor was in fear of losing his child. He cried out to the Lord for mercy, "God, if You are listening, please don't take my son! Please let him live!" Isn't it amazing how the church can be so wrong about our loving heavenly Father!

You never have to ask God to spare your life. He will never threaten you or your family with premature death. God is not going to "take you home" prematurely, when His will for you and your children is to have long life on the earth. The choice of life and death is not in the hands of God. He has given you the choice of life or death, blessing or curses: "I call heaven and earth as witness today against you, that I have set before you life and death, blessing and cursing; therefore choose life, that both you and your descendants may live" (Deuteronomy 30:19). You have been redeemed from the curse. If you want life and blessing, then choose life and blessing! When you choose to dwell in the secret place of the Most High, you have chosen life and blessing so that both you and your descendants may live.

No matter who is out to get you, the Lord will hide you underneath the shadow of His wings of protection.

CHAPTER 10

 C8

HIDING PLACE

You are my hiding place; You shall preserve me from trouble; You shall surround me with songs of deliverance. Selah.

Psalm 32:7

Have you ever been in trouble and felt like you had nowhere to run and nowhere to hide? You may have encountered trouble because of your own mistakes or foolish choices, or you may have been in deep distress because you did something right and were persecuted for righteousness' sake (Matthew 5:10). But then there were those other times in our past when the Lord's hand saved us from grave misfortune. Thank God for His mercy and His protection!

In David's lifetime, he made many wise choices, but he also made some very unwise decisions. He faced disaster due to his own mistakes, but he also faced persecution for righteousness' sake. One example of David's persecution was when his father-in-law, King Saul, sought to kill him out of fear and envy. Did I mention that David's father-in-law was also his employer? How would you like to go to work and have your boss throw a spear at your head? Talk about not getting along with your in-laws; David's "in-law" was more like an "outlaw"! There was nowhere David could hide in his country, since his father-in-law was king of the land. David found his hiding place under the wings of the Lord's protection.

Mikhtam Psalms

The book of Psalms has more to say about divine protection than any other book in the Bible. It is filled with blood covenant promises of divine protection. There are six Mikhtam Psalms in the book, found in chapters 16 and 56-60. The Mikhtam Psalms, also rendered "Golden Psalms," speak of David's trust in the Lord's protection and the deliverance He provided. For instance, Psalm 16 begins, "*Mikhtam. By David: Protect me, God, for you are my refuge. I said to ADONAI, 'You are my Lord; I have nothing good outside of you'*" (Psalm 16:1-2, CJB). David's words show he was entirely dependent upon the Lord's protection. David looked solely to Him as his safe haven.

In Psalm 56, David wrote of how he fled from King Saul and hid in Gath, the hometown of Goliath:

> *To the Chief Musician. Set to 'The Silent Dove in Distant Lands.' A Michtam of David when the Philistines captured him in Gath.*
>
> *Be merciful to me, O God, for man would swallow me up; fighting all day he oppresses me. My enemies would hound me all day, for there are many who fight against me, O Most High. Whenever I am afraid, I will trust in You. In God (I will praise His word), in God I have put my trust; I will not fear. What can flesh do to me?*
>
> Psalm 56:1-4

Have you ever felt like you were being hounded all day by someone who dislikes you? David was surrounded by his enemies in Gath. In fact, David was so fearful when facing King Achish of Gath that he pretended to be insane: "Now David took these words to heart, and was very much afraid of Achish the king of Gath" (1 Samuel 21:12). When David took the words of the enemy into his heart, he became very much afraid. But David put his trust in the Lord when he felt afraid. He called out for the Lord's protection and was delivered from all of his fears.

When you are in a major battle, that is not the time to fight back against your antagonist. That is the time to give praise for God's Word and place your trust in Him (Psalm 56:4). When you are trusting in the Lord to fight your battle, you no longer worry and you can say like David, "What can flesh do to me?" The Lord will protect you from flesh and blood oppressors.

Psalm 57 is a Mikhtam of David, written while he was hiding in a cave, praying for the Lord's divine protection: "To the Chief Musician. Set to 'Do Not Destroy.' A Michtam of David when he fled from Saul into the cave. Be merciful to me, O God, be merciful to me! For my soul trusts in You; and in the shadow of Your wings I will make my refuge, until these calamities have passed by" (Psalm 57:1).

When King Saul heard that David was in the Wilderness of En Gedi, Saul took 3,000 of his best soldiers to pursue him (1 Samuel 24:1-2). Place yourself in the shoes of David. Your father-in-law hates you so much that he hires 3,000 of the best mercenaries to kill you! How do you think you would sleep at night? Did you know that David was able to lie down and not be afraid? He chose to place his trust in the Lord and abide in His love.

David called the Lord's protection the "shadow of Your wings":

> *Be merciful [gracious] to me, God; be merciful [gracious] to me because I come to you for protection [seek refuge].*

Let me hide [be protected; seek refuge] under the shadow of your wings [Ruth 2:12; Matt. 23:37] until the trouble [destruction] has passed.

Psalm 57:1 EXB

This same metaphor is used in Psalm 91:4: "He shall cover you with His feathers, and under His wings you shall take refuge." It is also mentioned when the Lord reminds Israel how He delivered them on eagle's wings: "You have seen what I did to the Egyptians, and how I bore you on eagles' wings and brought you to Myself" (Exodus 19:4). David saw the Lord's protection as wings stretched out over him, giving him refuge from all his enemies.

Under the Shadow of His Wings

David wrote more about the Lord's divine protection than any other writer in the Bible. In Psalm 17, David speaks of how the Lord protected him as the apple of His eye.

I have called upon You, for You will hear me, O God; incline Your ear to me, and hear my speech. Show Your marvelous lovingkindness by Your right hand, O You who save those who trust in You from those who rise up against them. Keep me as the apple of Your eye; hide me under the shadow of Your wings, from the wicked who oppress me, from my deadly enemies who surround me.

Psalm 17:6-9

When you trust in the Lord as your hiding place, He will keep you as the apple of His eye. No matter who is out to get you, the Lord will hide you underneath the shadow of His wings of protection. The word "loving kindness" in this passage from Psalm 17 is translated from the Hebrew word *chesed*, which refers to the Lord showing goodness, favors, benefits, affection, and loving kindness in redemption from enemies and troubles, in preservation of life from death, in quickening of spiritual life, in redemption from sin, and in keeping the covenants.[18]   Notice that the loving kindness of the Lord's right hand will keep you protected from those who rise up against you.

David asked God to keep him as the apple of His eye. The expression "apple of your eye" refers to the natural inclination of a person to protect a vital organ such as his eye. This is the way God protects His own people. This prayer of David speaks to the close, intimate relationship he enjoyed with the Lord. When he speaks of the Lord's divine protection as hiding under the shadow of His wings, the imagery is of a young bird hiding underneath the protective wings of its mother. In the same way, you can find refuge in the Lord's arms.

Hidden in the Secret Place

> *One thing I have desired of the LORD, that will I seek: that I may dwell in the house of the LORD all the days of my life, to behold the beauty of the LORD, and to inquire in His temple. For in the time of trouble He shall hide me in His pavilion; in the secret place of His tabernacle He shall hide me; He shall set me high upon a rock.*

> Psalm 27:4-5

David's one desire was to dwell in the presence of the Lord all the days of his life. The word "desire" in the Hebrew is *sha'al*, which means "to ask, inquire, request, pray, desire, wish for, demand."[19]   This Hebrew word speaks not just of a casual request, but of an intense desire. David's desire to be in the presence of the Lord was intense. Over and above everything else, his heart was passionate about being in God's presence. There was nothing more important to David than being in fellowship with the Lord. This shows how David was a man after God's own heart (1 Samuel 13:14).

When King Saul's son Jonathan confirmed his father's plot to kill David, he encouraged David to flee to a hiding place: "My father Saul seeks to kill you. Therefore please be on your guard until morning, and stay in a secret place and hide" (1 Samuel 19:2). Where would you go if you received such a warning? David had nowhere to go except the secret place, where he found refuge in the Lord's protection. Time and again, David sought refuge in the Lord and the Lord faithfully protected him. When King Saul tried to pin David to the wall with his spear, David was able to escape unharmed (1 Samuel 19:10). When Saul endangered David's life by having him attack one hundred Philistines, David came back unharmed bearing two hundred foreskins of the Philistines (1 Samuel 18:25-28). Even King Saul had to recognize that the Lord was with David: "Thus Saul saw and knew that the LORD was with David" (1 Samuel 18:28).

Songs of Deliverance

After David was delivered from King Saul, he wrote songs of deliverance, speaking of the protection he found in the secret place.

> *Then David spoke to the LORD the words of this song, on the day when the LORD had delivered him from the hand of all his enemies, and from the hand of Saul. And he said: "The LORD is my rock and my fortress and my deliverer; the God of my strength, in whom I will trust; my shield and the horn of my salvation, my stronghold and my refuge; my Savior, You save me from violence."*

2 Samuel 22:1-3

Notice all the different ways David refers to the Lord as his protector in these few verses, calling Him…

"My rock"
"My fortress"
"My deliverer"

"My strength"
"My shield"
"My salvation"
"My stronghold"
"My refuge"
"My Savior"

The Lord was all of these to David. When David needed strength, he called on the Lord. When he needed a stronghold, he called on the Lord. When he needed a shield and a place of refuge, he called on the Lord. When you say of the Lord, "He is my refuge and my fortress; my God, in Him I will trust," that is what He will become to you. You can say like David, "You are my hiding place; You shall preserve me from trouble; You shall surround me with songs of deliverance. Selah" (Psalm 32:7).

Delivered from All Your Fears

When David escaped from King Saul, his worries were not over. He then encountered other enemies with whom he had to contend. In the title of Psalm 34, we see these words: "A Psalm of David when he pretended madness before Abimelech, who drove him away, and he departed" (Psalm 34:1). The title alludes to the instance when David approached Achish, the king of Gath, for refuge (1 Samuel 21:10). When the king of Gath recognized David he said, "Is this not David the king of the land? Did they not sing of him to one another in dances, saying: 'Saul has slain his thousands, and David his ten thousands'?" (1 Samuel 21:11). Upon hearing this, David changed his behavior, acting as a madman: "So he changed his behavior before them, pretended madness in their hands, scratched on the doors of the gate, and let his saliva fall down on his beard" (1 Samuel 21:13).

Why did David adopt such strange behavior? He was fearful. Fear will make you act like a madman. It will change your behavior. You will make all kinds of bad decisions when you are moved by fear. Ultimately, David was able to escape from Gath to the cave of Adullam because Achish, seeing David's behavior, believed that he was insane and of no threat to him (1 Samuel 21:14-22:1).

> *I sought the LORD, and He heard me, and delivered me from all my fears. They looked to Him and were radiant, and their faces were not ashamed. This poor man cried out, and the LORD heard him, and saved him out of all his troubles. The angel of the LORD encamps all around those who fear Him, and delivers them.*

Psalm 34:4-7

This passage tells us that the angel of the Lord "encamps all around those who fear Him." What is the fear of the Lord? Is it the phobia of God? Not at all. When you fear the Lord, you honor, reverence, and worship Him. David honored, reverenced and worshiped the Lord and the angel of the Lord surrounded him. When you fear the Lord, angels will surround you and cause your days to be prolonged: "The fear of the LORD prolongs days, but the years of the wicked will be shortened" (Proverbs 10:27).

David stated that the Lord delivered him from all his fears. On the cross, Jesus destroyed the devil, who had the power of death. Because of this triumph at the cross, Jesus is able to deliver us from *all* our fears, including the fear of death (Hebrews 2:14-15). The Lord delivered David from the fear of death and the fear of man. David no longer feared King Saul, nor King Achish of Gath. We are not to fear any man, but fear the Lord and honor those who are in authority (1 Peter 2:17). Consider these words written by the Apostle Paul to Pastor Timothy, which apply to us as well:

> *Therefore I remind you to stir up the gift of God which is in you through the laying on of my hands. For God has not given us a spirit of fear, but of power and of love and of a sound mind.*

2 Timothy 1:6-7

The Lord has not given you a spirit of fear. God himself lives on the inside of your recreated spirit (1 John 4:4). The power of the Holy Spirit resides inside you (Acts 1:8), you have the love of God inside your heart (Romans 5:5), and you have been given the mind of Christ (1 Corinthians 2:16). You no longer have to be in fear of anyone or anything when the Lord is your hiding place.

Divine Favor with Your Enemies

As King Saul's pursuit of David continued, David again went to the land of his enemies, the Philistines (1 Samuel 27). This was some time after David's initial encounter with Achish, king of the Philistines, when David was so fearful that he acted insane (1 Samuel 21:10-15). On this return to the land of his enemies, the Lord provided a hiding place for David while he dwelt there. Now that David had placed his trust in the Lord, he was able to face Achish in his right mind without any fear. The Lord had delivered David from all his fears.

You will encounter those who stand against you. They may hate you because of your faith in Christ or for other reasons. When I was in middle school, the entire student body was against me just because I came from the rival football town. No matter the situation, the Lord will cause your enemies to be at shalom with you, "When a man's ways please the LORD, He makes even his enemies to be at peace with him" (Proverbs 16:7). How do you please the Lord? You please Him by placing your trust in Him, by turning to Him as your refuge and reward (Hebrews 11:6).

In 1 Samuel 29, we see that the Philistine army was encamped in Aphek and David and his men were living among them. Keep in mind, Gath – the hometown of Goliath – was in the land of the Philistines. In fact, King Achish was the Philistine king of Gath. Now, on two different occasions, David has found refuge in Gath, the very hometown of Goliath, the giant David slew and decapitated (1 Samuel 17). Can you imagine this? Think about living in a country where everyone knows you are responsible for cutting off the head of their top military leader! Yet, David was able to sleep peaceably at night in the midst of his foes. He woke up every morning and had breakfast in the midst of the enemy: "Yea, though I walk through the valley of the shadow of death, I will fear no evil; for You are with me...You prepare a table before me in the presence of my enemies" (Psalm 23:4-5).

Just as He did for David, when you place your trust in the Lord as your hiding place, He will make your enemies to be at shalom with you (Proverbs 16:7). He will place before you a table of all of His benefits right in the midst of those who despise you (Psalm 23:5). When you place your trust in God, this pleases Him and He will surround you with divine favor as a shield of protection.

> *But let all those rejoice who put their trust in You; let them ever shout for joy, because You defend them; let those also who love Your name be joyful in You. For You, O LORD, will bless the righteous; with favor You will surround him as with a shield.*

> Psalm 5:11-12

When the Philistines were at war with Israel, the Philistine military leaders tried to convince King Achish to ask David to leave Gath. But the supernatural favor of God surrounded David and his men. King Achish commanded his military leaders to trust David and his men as allies: "Then the princes of the Philistines said, 'What are these Hebrews doing here?' And Achish said to the princes of the Philistines, 'Is this not David, the servant of Saul king of Israel, who has been with me these days, or these years? And to this day I have found no fault in him since he defected to me'" (1 Samuel 29:3).

Think about this for a moment. Achish, the Philistine king of Gath, hometown of Goliath, defended David to his military leaders. Remember, Goliath was the town hero. He was at one time the greatest warrior of the Philistine army. The Philistines named their newborn sons after Goliath. All the kids wore his number and jersey. Here is the king of the Philistines, showing favor to the one who beheaded their champion and carried his head around as a trophy. The one who humiliated the Philistines when he was just a Hebrew teenager. The king of Goliath's hometown showed David kindness and favor. This is supernatural favor and protection working together! When you make the Lord your hiding place, you can expect His favor to surround you as a shield in the midst of your adversaries.

Redeemed from Every Distress

In David's lifetime, he was not only pursued by the Philistines and King Saul, but also by his firstborn son, Absalom.

> *Now a messenger came to David, saying, "The hearts of the men of Israel are with Absalom." So David said to all his servants who were with him at Jerusalem, "Arise, and let us flee, or we shall not escape from Absalom. Make haste to depart, lest he overtake us suddenly and bring disaster upon us, and strike the city with the edge of the sword."*

2 Samuel 15:13-14

Absalom devised a plan to seize control of the kingdom from his father, starting in Hebron. As the plan started to unfold, David had to flee for his life (2 Samuel 2:13-17). In the end, Absalom's army was defeated by David's men and Absalom was killed. While riding on a mule, Absalom was caught by his long hair in the thick branches of a terebinth tree and David's men thrust three spears into his heart (2 Samuel 18:9). You might say that Absalom was having a bad hair day!

One of David's other sons, Adonijah, tried to overthrow David's heir to the throne, Solomon. Nathan the prophet warned Bathsheba, Solomon's mother, of the plot to kill both her and her son: "Come, please, let me now give you advice, that you may save your own life and the life of your son Solomon" (1 Kings 1:12). When David was made aware of the plot to kill both his wife and his son, he declared publicly right then that Solomon was the new king of Israel (1 Kings 1:30). Once David's chosen heir was safely in power, David praised God for the protection He had provided all the days of his life, "As the LORD lives, who has redeemed my life from every distress" (1 Kings 1:29).

There may be people close to you who want to hurt you, want you to go bankrupt, or even want you dead. Jesus understands what you are going through. Remember, His disciple Judas Iscariot betrayed Him and stole money out of His ministry (John 12:6). There may be close friends or family members who are envious of you or don't like you for whatever reason. They may have ill feelings toward you because of their own pride. They may hate you so badly that they would enjoy watching you get wiped out. Understand and know this - when you make the Lord your hiding place, they cannot touch you.

Your enemy is not your old boss, a former coworker, or an offensive neighbor. The only enemy you have is Satan. We do not wrestle against people but against principalities and powers of darkness in this world (Ephesians 6:12). Even though the enemy is out to destroy your life and make you suffer, he will not prevail. You can boldly declare the same thing David declared, "The Lord has redeemed my life from every distress."

Love Always Protects

David always showed King Saul God's mercy and kindness, even when Saul was pursuing him to kill him. David refused to harm King Saul (1 Samuel 24:10). David also refused to be offended at his son Absalom, who also tried to kill him. When David heard of Absalom's death, he wept bitter tears and cried, "O my son Absalom - my son, my son Absalom - if only I had died in your place! O Absalom my son, my son" (2 Samuel 18:33). David never saw Saul as his enemy, and he only saw Absalom as his dear son.

Love always protects and God, who is love, always protects His beloved in the secret place. Love always wins. When you refuse to get offended and choose to walk in the love of God, you will always win. You and your family will be kept safe, hidden, and protected from all strife.

> *For no man ever hated his own flesh, but nourishes and carefully protects and cherishes it, as Christ does the church.*

Ephesians 5:29, AMPC

> *It (the love of God) always protects, always trusts, always hopes, always perseveres. Love never fails.*

1 Corinthians 13:7-8, NIV, explanation mine

You cannot afford to have offense toward anyone, even those who have done you wrong. You will never go wrong when you choose to forgive, but things will always go wrong when you refuse to forgive. Let the unfailing love of Jesus fill your heart to help you to forgive. "Above all things have intense and unfailing love for one another, for love covers a multitude of sins [forgives and disregards the offenses of others]" (1 Peter 4:8, AMPC).

Hidden in the Secret Place

I love reading about the Pentecostal pioneers who blazed trails of world missions by their simple, raw faith in God's Word, His name, and the blood of Jesus. One of the greats was Assembly of God missionary Mrs. Cornelia Nuzum, who ministered for years to the Mexican people. Her faith in the blood covenant is evidenced in this account of a time she overcame the devil's attacks.

> This Blood avails for all things; it is our protection against everything if we will cry for it and trust in it. At one time I walked to a town about six miles distant, as the mules and horses were all away. On my way back I was some

distance from any house, when I saw a company of men sitting and drinking muscale (Mexican whiskey), and I saw they were becoming quite drunk with it. I left the path and circled around, but perceiving one of them had seen me and was coming after me as fast as he could, and was rapidly gaining on me at every step; I saw my danger and cried out for the Blood to protect me from this drunken man. Almost immediately his attention was attracted by some little thing along the road and he seemed to forget all about me.[20]

The drunken attacker was unable to get to Mrs. Nuzum because she was hidden in the secret place. When you cover yourself and your family with the blood of Jesus, the devil may seek to devour you, but he will not be able to find you. Why? The blood has hidden you in the secret place.

CHAPTER 11

BLOOD WARRIORS

David's fear of Achish, king of Gath, led him to flee to Adullam. It turns out, he was not the only one running to escape.

> David therefore departed from there and escaped to the cave of Adullam. So when his brothers and his entire father's house heard it, they went down there to him. And everyone who was in distress, everyone who was in debt, and everyone who was discontented gathered to him. So he became captain over them. And there were about four hundred men with him.

> 1 Samuel 22:1-2

David prayed for the Lord to take care of him and those who were near him - his family, friends, and those who had assembled with him. It states in 1 Samuel 22:2 that everyone who was in distress, in debt, and discontented gathered together in the cave of Adullam. You may be surrounded by people who fit that description. That may even describe your present condition, but it doesn't have to be that way. You can learn how to pray in a cave.

Prayer in a Cave

Just imagine, David was surrounded by 400 distressed, discontented people who also happened to be in debt. What do you think they wanted to do in the cave? I'm sure they had lots of conversations about the things that distressed them and left them discontented and in debt. That had all the makings of a depressing gathering. Imagine sitting in a dark, dreary cave with 400 discontented people talking about being in debt. But David knew how to pray in a cave. He knew how to encourage himself and others. His intimate relationship with the Lord kept him encouraged.

It's easy to pray on a mountaintop, but when you learn how to pray in a cave, then you've learned how to encourage yourself in the Lord's strength. These same 400 distressed, indebted, discontented people ended up becoming courageous "blood warriors" because they learned how to pray in the cave of Adullam.

A Maskil of David

Psalm 142 is a maskil psalm written by David when he was in the cave of Adullam. The Hebrew word maskil is translated "a contemplation" in the New King James translation of the Bible.

A Contemplation of David. A Prayer when he was in the cave.

I cried out to You, O Lord: I said, "You are my refuge, my portion in the land of the living.

Attend to my cry, for I am brought very low; Deliver me from my persecutors, for they are stronger than I.

*Bring my soul out of prison, that I may praise Your name;
The righteous shall surround me, for You shall deal
bountifully with me."*

Psalm 142:1, 5-7

David calls on the Lord for protection from those who would
lay a trap to take his life. Fear made David fainthearted and
depressed, nearly to the point that he saw no way of escape. He
knew that his enemies were too strong for him, so he prayed for
the Lord to save him by providing a place of refuge.

You may be able to relate to David. It may seem like there are
hidden traps set up to ensnare you. "It's only a matter of time and
you will fall again into my trap," says your adversary. So what do
you do when you feel lost, alone, and entrapped? David found
strength and refuge under the shadow of the Lord's wings.

Notice what David says in Psalm 142:5, "I cried out to You, O
LORD: I said, 'You are my refuge, my portion in the land of the
living.'" You may feel like you are stuck in a cave with no way
out, but this is not the end for you. You can cry out to God for
help. Place your trust in His protection and deliverance. When
you pray in a cave, He will surround you with songs of
deliverance.

*You are my hiding place; You shall preserve me from
trouble; You shall surround me with songs of deliverance.
Selah.*

Psalm 32:7

Praise and Prayer in the Prison

On their missionary journey, Paul and Silas traveled to Philippi,
a Roman colony. While they were there, the magistrates had them
thrown in jail for troubling the city (Acts 16:16-24). After they

had been severely beaten, Paul and Silas prayed and sang hymns to God while locked in the inner prison (Acts 16:25).

What do you think they prayed? If you had just been beaten and unjustly thrown into prison, what would you pray? My guess is just like Paul and Silas, you would pray for what you have need of – deliverance. And what do you think they sang about? They sang of God's deliverance and protection! Paul and Silas were praying and singing God's promises of deliverance. Suddenly, an earthquake shook the foundation of the prison, causing all the doors to open and all the prisoners' chains to fall off (Acts 16:26). This was a supernatural earthquake, a result of the prayer and praise that were offered by Paul and Silas while they were chained.

> *He shall call upon Me, and I will answer him; I will be with him in trouble; I will deliver him and honor him.*

> Psalm 91:15

Prior to the earthquake, the prisoners were all listening to Paul and Silas' prayers and hymns (Acts 16:25). Just imagine what it would have been like to be one of those prisoners. You see two new prisoners arrive - preachers who have just been beaten and mistreated. But they are not complaining over the dreadful conditions, nor are they making plans to escape. Instead, they are praying and singing of the Lord's deliverance.

When you dwell in the secret place, you always have prayer and praise in your mouth. Paul and Silas were praying according to God's promises of deliverance for His people.

> *"And I will make you to this people a fortified bronze wall; and they will fight against you, but they shall not prevail against you; for I am with you to save you and deliver you," says the LORD. "I will deliver you from the hand of the wicked, and I will redeem you from the grip of the terrible."*

> Jeremiah 15:20-21

The fact that the earthquake was powerful enough for every door of the prison to be opened and every prisoner's chains to fall off without one person being injured is an indication that this was a supernatural act of deliverance. Paul, Silas, and every prisoner remained inside the prison, unafraid and unharmed by the great earthquake (Acts 16:26-27). When you dwell in the secret place of the Lord, the chains of persecution and adversity will not be able to hold you. When you can pray and praise in a cave - or in a prison - the Lord will manifest His shalom.

I read an article in *USA Today* about a nine-year-old boy from Atlanta, Georgia, who was kidnapped from his driveway. The boy was trapped in the kidnapper's car for some time before the kidnapper dropped him off unharmed. It turns out that for three hours, the young boy sang the gospel song "Every Praise," by Hezekiah Walker. The kidnapper kept cursing at the boy, telling him to shut up and eventually, just kicked him out of the car. This boy had learned by the age of nine just how powerful prayer and praise can be.[21] When you can pray and praise in a cave, you will be preserved from trouble and surrounded with songs of deliverance (Psalm 32:7).

Blood Covenant Warriors

King David was one of the greatest warriors in the Bible. He faced and defeated armies, kings, giants, lions, and bears with supernatural strength and agility. His boldness and strength was a direct result of his intimate relationship with the Lord that began at an early age. David was so confident in the blood covenant that he dared to kill a lion by grabbing its beard and punching it in the face (1 Samuel 17:35). David's understanding of the blood covenant gave him a fearlessness to take on a 9-foot, 9-inch champion without wearing any armor (1 Samuel 17). He assured King Saul that Goliath would be defeated since he was a man without a blood covenant: "For who is this uncircumcised Philistine, that he should defy the armies of the living God?" (1 Samuel 17:26). Circumcision was the sign to Israel that they had a blood covenant with the living God. When David called Goliath an "uncircumcised Philistine," he was calling out the fact that Goliath had no blood covenant with the Almighty.

David's understanding of the blood covenant influenced his own band of militia, strengthening them to become mighty warriors. Remember, these were the "3-D" men who gathered to him in the cave who were in distress, in debt, and discontented (1 Samuel 22:2). But once they recognized their blood covenant with God and were supernaturally empowered, they became mighty warriors as strong as anything coming out of DC or Marvel superhero comics! Following David's example, they were strengthened by their blood covenant with the living God, "Now these were the heads of the mighty men whom David had, who strengthened themselves with him in his kingdom" (1 Chronicles 11:10). These men became strong and mighty in their blood covenant with the Lord as their source of strength, "For by You I can run against a troop; by my God I can leap over a wall" (2 Samuel 22:30). When you fully trust in the Lord as your strength, you will be able to run against anything that tries to take you down and leap over anything that may get in your way.

One of David's warriors, Adino, single handedly killed eight hundred men at one time (2 Samuel 23:8). Another one of David's mighty warriors was Eleazar, whose name means "God has helped."[22] Eleazar slaughtered an entire Philistine brigade with the help of the Lord: "He arose and attacked the Philistines until his hand was weary and his hand stuck to the sword. The LORD brought about a great victory that day" (2 Samuel 23:10).

Another one of David's mighty warriors was Shammah. When the Philistine army tried to steal his field full of lintels, Shammah stood his ground. Imagine being attacked by enemy troops coming to seize your property. One would probably be tempted to run away, but Shammah refused to hide in fear of the Philistines. Like David, he understood the Philistines were without a blood covenant with the living God. He stood in the middle of the field and defended it all by himself (2 Samuel 23:12). David's mighty warriors had learned how to receive supernatural strength by trusting in their blood covenant. You may be facing the adversary who has come to steal, kill, and destroy. Know that the Lord is with you. Station yourself in the middle of that situation fearlessly knowing that the victory is of the Lord's.

> The LORD does not save with sword and spear; for the battle is the LORD's.

1 Samuel 17:47

Facing an Army with One Weapon

I have members in my family who have served in the military. I have a great appreciation and honor for our veterans and soldiers who are willing to lay down their lives for the sake of our freedom. There are fascinating war stories all throughout the Old Testament, stories of great battles when Israel prevailed over insurmountable odds because they were under the shadow of the Lord in the secret place. When you read the many stories of Israel's victories, you always see the hand of God protecting His people.

One of the great soldiers of Israel's army was King Saul's son, Jonathan. In the second year Saul reigned over Israel, there was no blacksmith to be found in the land. The Philistines had prevented any blacksmiths from practicing their trade in Israel to ensure that the Israelites could not produce weapons, therefore, no one in Israel possessed a sword or spear, other than king Saul and his son Jonathan (1 Samuel 13:19, 22).

Though they had only one weapon between them, Jonathan decided to go over to the Philistine garrison with his armor bearer to see if the Lord would help them overthrow the army. The boldness of Jonathan to take on an entire army with only one sword was based on his belief in the Lord's divine protection: "Come let us go over to the garrison of these uncircumcised; it may be that the LORD will work for us. For nothing restrains the LORD from saving by many or by few" (1 Samuel 14:6). Jonathan understood that the angels of the Lord outnumbered the men of the

Philistine army. He believed his blood covenant with the Lord guaranteed that he would prevail over his enemies who were uncircumcised and without covenant.

When Jonathan and his armor bearer came against the Philistines, the Lord sent a supernatural earthquake that caused the Philistine army to fall into panic (1 Samuel 14:15). In their confusion, the Philistine army attacked one another using their own weapons (1 Samuel 14:20). The great earthquake that was sent from God brought divine deliverance to Israel: "So the LORD saved Israel that day and the battle shifted to Beth Aven" (1 Samuel 14:23). When you put your trust in the Lord's protection, He will cause your enemies to fall before your face (Deuteronomy 28:7). He knows how to put your enemies into panic so that their weapons cannot prevail against you (Isaiah 54:17).

Attacked in a Parking Lot

Lena and I experienced this supernatural protection when we were confronted with danger in a public parking lot. I had taken my wife to the hair salon and when we were told her hair dresser was running late, we decided to take a walk together in the back of the parking lot. We were holding hands, enjoying fellowship when suddenly, four men jumped out of a nearby pick-up truck screaming and threatening to hurt us. Lena and I were startled, wondering what we could have done to upset them. We noticed that these four men were all dressed in construction clothes. Apparently, these four angry men had just spent their day taring the parking lot in which we were walking, only to have us walk through it, leaving our tracks and marring their work. We hadn't realized we were walking over a freshly blacktopped parking lot. They were not happy construction workers!

All four men quickly came up behind us screaming violent and abusive threats. It looked like an apology would not do much good. These men didn't want an apology; they wanted one thing only – to hurt us both real bad!

We slowly walked away from the men as they continued to walk behind us shouting vicious threats. Tears started to fall down Lena's cheeks and she was shaking. All of a sudden, I stopped. I turned around and shouted, "STOP CRYING! THESE MEN CANNOT TOUCH US, IN JESUS' NAME! I COVER US WITH THE BLOOD OF JESUS!" As I said this, all four men stopped in their tracks. It was like confusion had come over them. It was comical to watch. They started to yell and shove each other and completely forgot all about us. It was like Lena and I had disappeared, just like when Jesus walked through the raging mob undetected: "Then passing through the midst of them, He went His way" (Luke 4:30). Lena and I looked at each other, smiled and walked away.

No weapon will work against you when you refuse to fear and instead, act on the blood covenant of protection: "In righteousness you shall be established; you shall be far from oppression, for you shall not fear; and from terror, for it shall not come near you" (Isaiah 54:14).

When you are in the secret place of the Lord's protection, you are hidden from the enemy. The Lord will make your enemies fall before your face: "The LORD will cause your enemies who rise against you to be defeated before your face; they shall come out against you one way and flee before you seven ways" (Deuteronomy 28:7). He will even cause His angels to chase your enemies into a dark and slippery path: "Let them be like chaff before the wind, and let the angel of the LORD chase them. Let their way be dark and slippery, and let the angel of the LORD pursue them" (Psalm 35:5-6).

Blood Warriors in the Last Days

It seems things in this world's society have become darker and more dangerous than in any other generation. Satan knows his time is short and has unleashed his great wrath on this world.

Woe to the inhabitants of the earth and the sea! For the devil has come down to you, having great wrath, because he knows that he has a short time.

Revelation 12:12

God is revealing in these last days how to dwell underneath His wings as our place of refuge. He has given us access to the secret place so we can live safely in perilous times. You do not have to be afraid of anything or anyone. You have been given dominion over darkness.

The spirit of terrorism and demonic violence has been spreading all over our world. The driving force behind these acts is the spirit of fear. Death and destruction have been manifested in recent mass shootings in public places such as churches, movie theaters, military posts, and schools. But the Church has been given dominion over demon spirits. We are the only ones who have been given authority; we are in charge. We must not see ourselves any longer as "church mice" - we are called to be mighty blood warriors of the blood covenant. This is why it is so vital for you to understand your blood covenant of divine protection, that you might become a blood warrior in your family, your church, your city, and your nation.

Over the years, Lena and I have ministered in numerous evangelism outreaches in various areas of South Florida. We always start each outreach by praying Psalm 91 and covering everyone in the outreach team with the blood of Jesus. One time while we were sharing the good news in Miami, we encountered some opposition. As we crossed over to the other side of a neighborhood, we heard loud shouting and noticed a group of young men in a large circle. As we came towards them, we prayed in the Spirit for direction and utterance. One of the young men saw us coming and quickly ran up to me and warned, "You need to leave our neighborhood! You don't know who you're dealin' with!" The Holy Spirit came upon me with boldness and I told all of them to stop for a moment and listen. I stood in the middle of their circle where they had been rolling dice and gambling large amounts of cash. I informed them that I did not plan to waste my afternoon and I expected every one of them to listen. I simply preached the saving gospel of Jesus to these men and not religion. The young man who earlier had warned me to leave allowed me to lay hands on him and pray over him. Some of the men had tears in their eyes as I laid hands on them and prayed. I told them that one day, they would be the ones preaching the good news of the gospel to their neighborhood. All twenty men bowed their heads and received Christ Jesus as their Lord and Savior.

On another outreach, Lena and I encountered two young men who laughed at us as we went through their neighborhood sharing the good news. Lena handed one of them a gospel tract and told him, "Here you go. Jesus loves you." He took the tract, threw it on the ground, stomped on it and mockingly said, "Jesus loves me! Jesus loves me!" Lena refused to get offended and blessed the young man as she walked away.

The young man was in awe at the love of Jesus shining through Lena as he watched her walk away. All of a sudden, he picked the tract up off the ground, hurriedly got on his bicycle and caught up to Lena, asking for her forgiveness. He shared with her that his mother was seriously ill and he had been very upset about it. Lena prayed for his mother to be healed and the young man received Christ Jesus as his Lord and Savior. Darkness does not have the upper hand. The Church has been given dominion and has the upper hand of authority.

We are in a war with the enemy of fear, death, disaster, and destruction. God has called us to overcome by the blood of the Lamb and the word of our testimony (Revelation 12:11). It is up to us to take our God-given dominion, place our trust in the Lord's blood covenant and become His blood warriors in these perilous times.

NO WEAPON

NO WEAPON CONFESSION

Declare with boldness who you are in Christ Jesus:

"I am in Christ Jesus and I am a new creation; old things have passed away; and ALL things have become new.
2 Corinthians 5.17

I am the righteousness of God in Christ Jesus.
2 Corinthians 5.21

I have been justified by faith in the Blood of Jesus.
Romans 5.9

I have peace with God through my Lord Jesus Christ, and I stand by faith in this grace.
Romans 5.1-2

I have received the abundance of grace, And the free gift of righteousness.
Romans 5.17

I reign in this life through the One, Jesus Christ.
Romans 5.17

There is therefore now, no condemnation, for I am in Christ Jesus.
Romans 8.1

And the law of the Spirit of life in Christ Jesus, has made me free from the law of sin and death.
Romans 8.2

For sin shall not have dominion over me, for I am not under law but under grace.
Romans 6.14

I have not received the spirit of bondage to fear
But I have received the spirit of adoption by whom I cry out
Daddy, Father God.
Romans 8.15

The Spirit Himself bears witness with my spirit that
I am a child of God.
Romans 8.16

I am an heir of God, and I am joint heirs with Christ Jesus.
Romans 8.17

Father God is for me and not against me.
Romans 8.31

My Father loves me as much as He loves Jesus.
John 15.9

I am born of God and I overcome the world.
1 John 4.4

I have the victory that overcomes the world, my faith.
1 John 5.4

I believe as He is so am I in this world.
1 John 4.17

Jesus has forgiven me from ALL sins
and He remembers them no more.
Hebrews 8.12

I am washed in the Blood of Jesus.
He has made a king and priest."
Revelation 1.6

"I am righteous, Romans 5.1

redeemed, Ephesians 1.7

perfected, Hebrews 10.14

purified, Hebrews 9.14

protected, 1 John 5.18

prosperous, 2 Corinthians 8.9

healed, 1 Peter 2.24

sealed, Ephesians 1.13

sanctified, Hebrews 10.10

spotless, 2 Peter 3.14

seated, Ephesians 2.6

His son, Galatians 3.26

complete, Colossians 2.10

clean, 1 John 1.7

accepted, Romans 15.7

justified, Romans 5.1

free, John 8.36

I am a friend of God, John 15.15

Forgiven," Colossians 1.14

"His beloved, Romans 1.7

blameless, Philippians 2.15

bold as a lion, Proverbs 28.1

and I am BLESSED! Ephesians 1.3

I am an overcomer,
and I overcome the accuser of the brethren,
by the Blood of the Lamb and by the Word of my testimony!
Revelation 12.11

No weapon formed against me shall prosper
and every tongue which rises against me in judgment
I condemn, and show to be in the wrong!
Isaiah 54.17 AMPC

This is my heritage, my inheritance, and my Blood Covenant!"
Ephesians 1.11

PRAYER OF PROTECTION

Take the blood covenant of divine protection and verbally declare these things by faith.

In the name of Jesus, I cover myself, my spouse, my children, every member of my family, all my possessions, my church, my friends, my neighborhood, my city, and the nation's governing authority with the blood of Jesus.

I declare that we dwell in the secret place of the Most High. We abide under the shadow of the Almighty. I will say of the Lord, He is our refuge and our fortress; He is our God, and in Him we will trust.

Surely He shall deliver us from the snare of the fowler and from the perilous pestilence. He shall cover us with His feathers, and under His wings we shall take refuge; His truth is our shield and buckler.

We shall not be afraid of the terror by night, nor of the arrow that flies by day, nor of the pestilence that walks in darkness, nor of the destruction that lays waste at noonday.

A thousand may fall at our side, and ten thousand at our right hand; but it shall not come near us. Only with our eyes we shall look, and see the reward of the wicked.

Because we have made the Lord who is our refuge, even the Most High, our dwelling place, no evil shall befall us, nor shall any plague come near our dwelling;

for He shall give His angels charge over us, to keep us in all our ways. In their hands they shall bear us up, lest we dash our foot against a stone.

We shall tread upon the lion and the cobra, the young lion and the serpent we shall trample underfoot.

Because we have set our love upon Him, therefore He will deliver us; He will set us on high, because we know His name.

We shall call upon Him, and He will answer us; He will be with us in trouble and will deliver us and honor us. With long life He will satisfy us, and show us His salvation.

Amen.

- Psalm 91, paraphrased

FINAL WORDS

I pray that this book has helped you receive a fresh revelation and understanding of your inheritance of divine protection in Christ Jesus. It is an honor for me to share these truths with you. As you abide in the secret place of the Most High, you will experience the supernatural protection of the blood covenant. I would love to hear about your experience and look forward to receiving your testimonies of supernatural protection. You can contact our ministry by visiting our website at *harvesti.org*.

May God's grace and shalom be multiplied to you and your entire family, in Jesus' name. Amen.

PRAYER OF SALVATION

No one has been made right before God through their own efforts. Everyone has sinned and fallen short of God's standards of perfection: "For all have sinned and fall short of the glory of God" (Romans 3:23). Jesus is the only one who fully and perfectly fulfilled all the requirements of the law. You are not right with God because of any righteous acts you have done; He considers them like filthy rags covered in human blood (Isaiah 64:6). The only way you can be right with God is to accept His free gift of righteousness through faith in the blood of His Son, Jesus: "Therefore, having been justified by faith, we have peace with God through our Lord Jesus Christ" (Romans 5:1).

If you have never called on Jesus to be your Lord and Savior, today is the day of salvation. I invite you to pray this prayer aloud from your heart:

Jesus, I am a sinner and I am in need of a Savior.

I believe You are the Son of God. I believe You died on the cross and shed Your blood for me.

I believe God raised You from the dead. I believe You are seated at His right hand in heaven.

I receive Your forgiveness of all my sins.

God, You are my Father.

Jesus, You are my Lord and Savior.

Holy Spirit, You live on the inside of me. Fill me with Your power as I yield myself to You.

In Jesus' name, Amen!

ABOUT THE AUTHOR

Dr. Brian Miltenberger is a Bible teacher, pastor, and founder of Harvest International. His calling is to reach the world with the good news of Jesus Christ.

For over twenty-five years, Dr. Miltenberger has been preaching and teaching the Word of God with the demonstration of the power of the Holy Spirit in church services, conferences, Bible schools, radio, youth ministry, outreaches, prisons, and internationally.

His messages of faith and grace declare that Father God is good and His mercy endures forever.

Dr. Brian Miltenberger, his wife Lena, and their two children live in South Florida. For more information on Dr. Brian Miltenberger please visit harvesti.org.

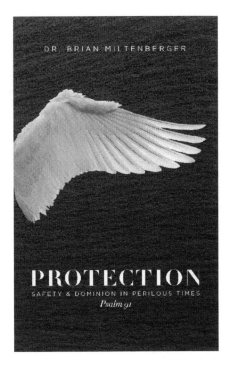

PROTECTION

SAFETY & DOMINION IN PERILOUS TIMES

We are living in the last days of perilous times. We are bombarded daily with bad news about the latest murder, car accident, plane crash, missing child, terrorist threat, mass shooting, life threatening virus, or natural disaster.

It seems no place is exempt from danger. There is a widespread fear of sudden death, unexpected danger, and unavoidable tragedy. In these last days, God is revealing to His people how to live free from fear, even though we live in a world full of menace. You can keep safe in dangerous times! Learn how to live free from the fear of danger always abiding safe in the secret place of protection.

NOTES

Chapter One

[1] John MacArthur. *The MacArthur New Testament Commentary: Matthew 1-7* (Chicago, Illinois: The Moody Bible Institute of Chicago, 1985), 26.

[2] Ibid.

[3] Joseph H. Thayer. *Thayer's Greek-English Lexicon of the New Testament* (Grand Rapids, Michigan: Baker Book House, 1977), 64.

Chapter Two

[4] James Strong. *Exhaustive Concordance of the Bible* (Peabody, Massachusetts: Hendrickson Publishers, 2009), Strong's Number 7965.

W.E. Vine. *Vine's Complete Expository Dictionary of the Old Testament Words* (Nashville, Tennessee: Thomas Nelson Publishers, 1985), 173.

Chapter Three

[5] James Strong. *Exhaustive Concordance of the Bible* (Peabody, Massachusetts: Hendrickson Publishers, 2009), Strong's Number 8104.

[6] Note from *Faithlife Study Bible* (Bellingham, Washington: Lexham Press. Logos Bible Software, 2012), 23.

[7] Merrill F. Unger and William White, Jr. *Nelson's Expository Dictionary of the Old Testament* (Nashville, Tennessee: Thomas Nelson Publishers, 1980), 16.

Robert Baker Girdleston. *Synonyms of the Old Testament* (Grand Rapids, Michigan: W.M. Eerdmans Publishing Company, 1897), 128.

[8] Joan Comay and Ronald Brownrigg. *Who's Who In the Bible: Two Volumes in One* (New York, New York: Bonanza Books, 1980), 302.

[9] Note from *The Spirit Filled Life Study Bible (SFB), New King James Version* (Nashville, Tennessee: Thomas Nelson Publishers, 1991), 1855.

Chapter Five

[10] Note from *The Spirit Filled Life Study Bible (SFB). New King James Version* (Nashville, Tennessee: Thomas Nelson Publishers, 1991), 1260.

Chapter Six

[11] Joan Comay and Ronald Brownrigg. *Who's Who In the Bible: Two Volumes in One* (New York, New York: Bonanza Books, 1980), 235.

[12] Ibid., 167.

[13] Warren Baker, D.R.E. and Eugene Carpenter, Ph.D. *The Complete Word Study Dictionary: Old Testament* (Chattanooga, Tennessee: AMG Publishers, 2003), 1722.

Chapter Eight

[14] Terry Mize. *More Than Conquerors* (Tulsa, Oklahoma: Harrison House, 1979), 13-14.

[15] Ibid., 16.

[16] Ibid., 18.

Chapter Nine

[17] Joan Comay and Ronald Brownrigg. *Who's Who In the Bible: Two Volumes in One* (New York, New York: Bonanza Books, 1980), 63.

Chapter Ten

[18] Francis Brown, S.R. Driver and Charles A. Briggs. *The Brown-Driver-Briggs Hebrew and English Lexicon* (Peabody, Massachusetts: Hendrickson Publishers, 2000), 338-339.

[19] James Strong. *Exhaustive Concordance of the Bible* (Peabody, Massachusetts: Hendrickson Publishers, 2009), Strong's Number 7592 and note from *The Spirit Filled Life Study Bible (SFB), New King James Version* (Nashville, Tennessee: Thomas Nelson Publishers, 1991), 863.

[20] Cornelia Nuzum. *The Life of Faith* (Gospel Publishing House, 1928 and 1956), 57-58.

Chapter Eleven

[21] Blayne Alexander, "Boy released by kidnapper after singing gospel music," *USA Today.com,* April 23, 2016, https://www.usatoday.com/story/news/nation-now/2014/04/23/gospel-singing-kidnapping/8042195/.

[22] Joan Comay and Ronald Brownrigg. *Who's Who In the Bible: Two Volumes in One* (New York, New York: Bonanza Books, 1980), 107.

Made in the USA
Monee, IL
23 September 2020

42467962R20083